After Efficiency

Building a Career Machines Can't Replace

Pierre TELEP

First Edition: January 2026

ISBN 978-3-9828263-0-1

DEDICATION

For those who create value through their work, their care, their creativity.

For those who choose wisdom over mere intelligence.

For those who build things that matter and make the world incrementally better through countless small choices.

Contents

Introduction

We are living in an age where intelligence is no longer the sole domain of humans. Machines can learn, adapt, predict, and even create. Artificial Intelligence (AI) is no longer a force of the future. It is here, deeply woven into our daily routines, our economies, and our imaginations.

On social media, we can no longer be sure whether we're interacting with a person or a digital entity. In our workplaces, algorithms make decisions, filter applicants, generate reports, and even suggest our next moves. The music we stream is increasingly composed, remixed, or curated by AI systems trained on vast datasets of human taste. Humanoids are now being developed to interact with people in ways that not only replicate human behavior, but simulate emotional presence.

One can foresee a world, not far from now, where digital beings might not just support us, but stand beside us in nearly every sphere of life: as coworkers, advisors, even companions. Though this is scary for many, the reality is that AI is no longer emerging. It has arrived, and it is accelerating.

And yet, amidst this rising tide of algorithmic precision, automated creation, and cognitive outsourcing, some fundamental questions are worth exploring:

1. What is value today, and in the near future?

In this age of AI and data-driven decision making and performance, what does value mean? Is it just about the final product, the productivity or performance that led to it, or the quality of the product? Or is there a shifting and dynamic pattern of value creation that we need now to understand?

2. What does it mean to create value in the time of AI?

If machines can now learn, produce, and even *"innovate,"* what space remains for human creativity and contribution? How do we reimagine our role, not just as users of AI, but as co-creators of intelligent systems that serve real human needs?

3. What are the existential implications of value in a machine-augmented world?

As we entrust more of our decision-making and creation to artificial systems, how do we preserve our sense of dignity, purpose, and meaning? What makes our existence valuable, not just to the system, but to ourselves and to each other?

Why This Book? Why Now?

As a consultant and founder of Climate Platform, I've spent my career working at the crossroads of sustainability, innovation, and global development. My mission has been clear, though not simple: to help communities, institutions, and organizations not just understand the complex realities of climate change, but to respond with solutions that are scalable, meaningful, and rooted in impact.

Recently a client called with news that shook me. AI has now entered climate consulting specialties, they said, and because they enjoyed working with me, they wanted to give me a heads up. I might soon become irrelevant to the market. The advice came at the right time.

While advising governments on climate finance strategies and supporting private sector innovators in building resilience through technology these past years, I've come to observe changing patterns. The traditional definitions of value (profit, performance, efficiency) are no longer enough. In a world increasingly shaped by AI and existential challenges, we need new maps for meaning, new metrics for what matters, and new languages for leadership.

This book is my attempt to offer a compass. It is for those who are not content to merely survive the future, but to shape it consciously.

Who This Is For

This book is for you if you're a professional quietly wondering whether your work will still matter in a year, or in a world run by algorithms. It's for the entrepreneur building something new, hoping their idea can still stand out when machines are getting better at everything. It's for leaders who want to build more than just systems. They want to build human-centered, resilient futures.

And if you're a student, a thinker, or just someone trying to make sense of this fast-changing reality with your integrity intact, this is your space too.

If you care about what matters, what endures, and what uplifts, you're in the right place.

The Promise of This Book

In the pages ahead, we'll take a journey into how AI is reshaping the very nature of value. What it enhances, what it replaces, and just as importantly, what it cannot touch. Along the way, we'll explore why qualities like empathy, ethics, and the ability to genuinely serve others are becoming more valuable than ever. Perhaps even the new premium.

You'll discover ways to grow your skills, shape your mindset, and build projects that not only keep pace with the future, but stay rooted in your deepest values. By the end of this book, you'll be equipped to redefine, recognize, and generate true value in an AI-driven world that's evolving by the day.

Because this isn't just a book about technology. It's a book about truth, transformation, and the kind of human potential that never goes out of date.

PART I

The Nature of Value in the Age of Artificial Intelligence

Chapter 1

What is Value ? Who Defines It?

The Evolution of Value: From Ancient Societies to the AI Age

The idea of value (what is considered worthwhile, useful, or worthy of exchange) has never been static. Across cultures and eras, societies have defined value through the lens of their dominant economic, spiritual, and technological realities. From sacred grains to digital code, the story of value is a mirror of how humans have related to labor, resources, power, and meaning.

1. Value in Babylonian and Ancient Egyptian Societies

In early civilizations like Babylonia and ancient Egypt, value was deeply embedded in religion, agriculture, and social order. Grains, livestock, and land were common units of value, not just as commodities but as symbols of divine favor and societal role. Temples acted as both spiritual centers and economic institutions, collecting offerings, redistributing goods, and even issuing early forms of credit.

Labor held value insofar as it contributed to religious rituals, agricultural cycles, and royal projects like pyramid building or canal maintenance. Here, value was less about market logic and more about function, hierarchy, and cosmic balance. What mattered was not what something could fetch in trade, but what role it played in maintaining the divine and social order.

2. Value from Antiquity to 600 AD

In classical Greece and Rome, value shifted toward trade and exchange. Currency systems developed, and value became increasingly tied to precious metals and exchangeable goods. Philosophers like Aristotle made early distinctions between use value and exchange value, laying the groundwork for later economic theory.

Still, the economy remained grounded in labor-intensive production, slavery, and land ownership. Wealth signaled power, but value remained tied to what something could do or command in return. A sword had value not just for its iron and craftsmanship, but for the power it conferred on its wielder.

3. Value in the Medieval to Pre-Industrial Era (600–1700)

During the medieval period, value took on a moral and theological dimension. In Christian Europe, for instance, the Church viewed profit-seeking with suspicion, and usury (charging interest) was condemned. Economic value was closely linked to social function and divine order. A blacksmith's work was valuable not because it was profitable, but because it served the community. Guilds regulated the quality and fairness of trade. Value here was communal, ethical, and functional, not primarily driven by market mechanisms.

In Islamic societies, commerce was more robustly embraced, but with a strong ethical framework defined by the Quran and Hadith. In both traditions, the human role in creating value was guided by spiritual accountability. The question wasn't simply *"What can I gain?"* but *"Am I fulfilling my responsibilities to God and community?"*

4. Value in the Industrial Era (1700s–1900s)

The Industrial Revolution radically redefined value. Mass production, urbanization, and mechanized labor shifted the focus from craftsmanship to output and efficiency. It was in this era that economists like Adam Smith formalized value theory.

In The Wealth of Nations (1776), Smith wrote:

"The real price of everything, what everything really costs to the man who wants to acquire it, is the toil and trouble of acquiring it."

Smith introduced the labor theory of value, asserting that a commodity's true worth lies in the labor required to produce it under normal conditions. However, he was also pragmatic, recognizing that in complex economies, market prices are shaped by wages, profit, and rent, the three elements he described as components of the *"natural price."*

Smith added:

"The market price of every particular commodity is regulated by the proportion between the quantity which is actually brought to market, and the demand of those who are willing to pay...the natural price...is, as it were, the central price."

This marked a significant evolution: value was no longer simply embedded in objects or their moral utility. It became a function of production, labor input, and market dynamics. For the first time, value could be calculated, optimized, and maximized through systematic analysis.

5.   Value in the Internet Era (1990s–2020s)

With the rise of the internet and digital technologies, value once again shifted. This time from physical goods and manual labor to data, connectivity, and network effects. Information became a commodity. Companies like Google, Facebook, and Amazon built trillion-dollar empires not by owning physical factories, but by controlling attention, access, and algorithms.

In this era, data became a form of labor, but not in the traditional sense. Every click, like, and search contributes to value creation, often invisibly. Unlike the laborers of the industrial age, today's *"value creators"* often don't know they're working. Their behavior, preferences, and personal information are extracted, processed, and monetized, raising profound questions about ownership, consent, and what it truly means to create value in the digital age.

The power dynamics shifted too. Value was no longer determined primarily by those who produced goods, but by those who controlled platforms and algorithms. A musician could create brilliant work, but if the algorithm didn't surface it, it might as well not exist.

6.   Value in the AI Age (2020s–Present)

We have now entered what could be the most profound shift in the story of value since the invention of money: the AI Age. Here, value as we've known it before is increasingly generated by intelligent systems capable of learning, predicting, creating content, and even making decisions. Tasks once considered the sole domain of human cognition.

AI-powered platforms now write reports, compose music, diagnose diseases, and trade stocks, blurring the lines between human and machine-generated work. For the first time, we must ask: Can value be created without human presence? If an AI can produce a painting, solve a legal dispute, or provide therapy, where does that leave the human contributor?

In this era, value is decoupling from direct labor. It emerges from architecture, access, algorithms, and outcomes, often invisible to the user. Companies no longer extract value from natural resources alone, but from the behavior, creativity, and vulnerabilities of people mediated through digital systems.

This raises urgent questions: Who owns the value created by AI trained on human data? When an algorithm composes music using patterns learned from thousands of human musicians, who deserves credit? When an AI system makes decisions that affect people's lives, who bears responsibility?

The Three Dimensions of Value: Perception, Utility, and Impact

To truly understand value, especially in today's AI-driven world, we need to look beyond numbers, profits, or market buzz. Value is a multidimensional concept, and at its core, it's shaped by three distinct but interwoven forces: perception, utility, and impact.

Perception: How Value Is Seen

Perception is all about how something is seen or felt by others. It's influenced by branding, reputation, media attention, and even the charisma of the person delivering it. A luxury handbag may have the same function as a simple tote, but its perceived value is worlds apart, thanks to the name stamped on it.

Perception shapes what people are willing to pay, who they trust, and what they consider prestigious or worthwhile. It's why a painting by a famous artist sells for millions while a technically superior work by an unknown painter goes unnoticed. It's why a doctor's diagnosis feels weightier than the same diagnosis from an AI, even when the AI might be more accurate.

In the AI age, perception becomes both more malleable and more critical. AI can generate content that looks professional, sounds authoritative, and appears competent. But can it generate the perception of authenticity, trustworthiness, and genuine care? That remains an open question.

Utility: How Value Functions

Utility is about practical usefulness. It's the function something serves, whether it solves a problem, fills a need, or makes life easier. A public transit app that helps people get to work on time may have incredible utility, even if it's not glamorous or hyped.

Utility is the most objective dimension of value. You can measure it, test it, and verify it. Does the tool work? Does it deliver the promised outcome? Does it make the task easier, faster, or better?

AI excels at delivering utility. It can process information faster, identify patterns more comprehensively, and execute tasks more consistently than humans. This is why AI adoption is accelerating across industries. The utility is undeniable.

But utility alone doesn't tell the whole story. A medication might be highly effective (high utility) but if people don't trust it or can't afford it, its value is limited. A tool might be powerful but if it's too complex for people to use, its practical value diminishes.

Impact: How Value Reverberates

Impact is the often overlooked but arguably most important dimension. Impact is about consequence: What effect does something have on people, society, or the planet? A technology that helps reduce carbon emissions might not trend on social media, but its long-term impact could be massive.

Impact considers not just immediate effects but ripple effects. Second-order consequences. Long-term implications. A decision that optimizes for short-term profit might have negative long-term impact on employee wellbeing, community health, or environmental sustainability.

This is where human judgment becomes essential. AI can optimize for defined metrics, but it cannot weigh competing values, consider unintended consequences, or make ethical trade-offs in novel situations. It cannot ask whether the impact we're creating is the impact we should create.

When the Three Dimensions Align (and When They Don't)

Sometimes, these three dimensions align beautifully. A product is seen as valuable, it works well, and it creates positive change. When this happens, you have sustainable value creation that serves all stakeholders.

But often, they don't align. Consider these examples:

An AI-powered mental health app might be incredibly useful (high utility) and capable of improving lives (positive impact), yet struggle with poor perception due to concerns over privacy or the stigma of seeking help from a machine rather than a human therapist.

A celebrity influencer may have sky-high perceived value (millions of followers, lucrative sponsorships), but the advice they offer, often boosted by AI-generated content, can be shallow or even harmful (negative impact), especially if it drives overconsumption, spreads misinformation, or promotes unrealistic standards.

Soil regeneration techniques in agriculture have the potential for massive environmental and economic impact, especially for smallholder farmers (high impact, significant utility). But because they're not trendy or easy to monetize quickly, they often receive little attention or investment (low perception), limiting their adoption.

Understanding value requires dissecting all three dimensions:

Perception: How individuals or societies perceive the worth of a product, service, or idea.

Utility: The practical usefulness of a product, service, or idea; its ability to fulfill a need.

Impact: The broader consequences of a product, service, or idea, including social, environmental, and economic effects.

These three dimensions will appear throughout this book as we explore how to create genuine value in the AI age. The most successful individuals and organizations will be those who learn to build offerings that score high across all three dimensions, not just one or two.

Human vs. Machine-Created Value: A New Equation

The rise of AI has fundamentally shifted how we think about who (or what) creates value. From writing emails to composing music, from diagnosing illnesses to designing business strategies, machines are now stepping into arenas once considered exclusively human.

But the value created by machines is not the same as that created by people. To understand this difference, we need to look at it through the lens of our three dimensions: perception, utility, and impact.

Perception: Who Do We Trust?

AI can generate impressive outputs, but public perception often lags behind performance. A beautifully written article by a language model may be seen as clever or eerie, but not *"authentic."* In contrast, even a flawed message from a human can carry emotional weight, context, and intention.

People still perceive human-generated value as more personal, responsible, and trustworthy, especially in areas involving ethics, care, or leadership. We want to know there's a human being who can be held accountable, who genuinely cares about the outcome, who brings moral judgment to bear.

This perception gap creates opportunity. In a world flooded with AI-generated content, the provably human becomes premium. The handwritten note. The personal phone call. The leader who shows up in person during a crisis. These carry perceived value precisely because they require human presence and intention.

Utility: Who Gets the Job Done?

When it comes to efficiency and precision, machines often outperform us. They can process vast datasets, detect patterns in seconds, and never get tired. AI delivers clear utility, especially in repetitive, data-driven, or technical tasks.

A radiologist might spend hours reviewing scans; an AI can review thousands in the same time. A legal researcher might need days to find relevant precedents; an AI can surface them in minutes. For pure utility in defined tasks, AI increasingly wins.

But humans bring something else: adaptive intelligence. Where conditions are ambiguous or rapidly changing, human intuition, creativity, and emotional intelligence remain irreplaceable. When the problem itself is unclear, when context matters profoundly, when the situation has never been encountered before, human utility still exceeds machine utility.

The sweet spot is combining both: AI for scale and consistency, humans for judgment and adaptation.

Impact: What Are the Long-Term Consequences?

Here's where things get truly complex. An AI might solve a problem today but create new ethical or social issues tomorrow. Unemployment from automation. Bias embedded in algorithms. Erosion of trust when people can't distinguish human from machine. Privacy violations from data harvesting. The concentration of power in the hands of those who control AI systems.

Human decision-making, though slower, is informed by values, relationships, and context. Long-term impact depends not just on what we build, but how we build it and why.

Machines don't wrestle with questions of meaning or morality. They optimize for defined objectives without questioning whether those objectives serve human flourishing. We do. Or at least, we can. And in the AI age, this capacity becomes our most important contribution.

Recognizing these distinctions across perception, utility, and impact is crucial in determining how to integrate AI into various professions and domains without compromising the unique value humans offer. It's not about humans versus machines. It's about understanding what each contributes and orchestrating their collaboration wisely.

As we move into Chapter 2, we'll explore how this dynamic plays out across different professions, examining where human value remains essential and where augmentation creates possibilities neither humans nor machines could achieve alone.Claude is AI and can make mistakes. Please double-check responses.

Chapter 2

Value Creation Across Professions: A Three-Dimensional View

It is no longer speculative. Machines are not only performing tasks once reserved for human experts, they are learning, adapting, and improving at a rate that challenges our traditional ideas of professional value. The AI era is here now, and it requires us to rethink the very principle of value creation.

Here are some examples of professions where our three dimensions of value (perception, utility, and impact) play out in revealing ways.

Consultants and Strategic Advisors

Consultants provide strategic advice to organizations, helping them navigate complex challenges. AI can already analyze data faster than any human team, model complex scenarios, and recommend evidence-based strategies with increasing sophistication. The utility is not just high, it's accelerating.

Perception is also shifting. As clients become more comfortable with AI-generated insights and as algorithmic outputs grow more persuasive and personalized, the perceived value of machine-generated advice could rival or even surpass that of human consultants, especially when costs and speed are factored in.

Impact, too, may lean toward machines in certain contexts. A data-driven policy generated by AI could prevent financial loss or improve system efficiency far beyond what a human advisor might achieve.

Now, despite the exponential rise in machine capability, many clients still choose to work with human consultants. Why? Not necessarily because humans are faster (they're not), or because they can analyze more data (they can't), but because human consultants offer something subtler, yet deeply valued: interpersonal insight, emotional intelligence, and ethical framing. Their recommendations are shaped not only by information, but by intuition, context, and care.

AI, for all its speed and scale, still lacks the nuanced ability to read a room, navigate unspoken tensions, or understand the ripple effects of a decision across a community's lived experience. And yet, this might not always be the case. In a world where AI is gaining credibility and capability, and as hiring decisions themselves are increasingly made or influenced by algorithms, it becomes clear that when selecting consultants based purely on performance metrics, speed, and cost, an AI system could very well choose itself or its peer.

The amount of things that humans can offer that machines can't is decreasing. And in this changing landscape, the role of the human consultant or expert advisor must quickly evolve. Competing on speed, scale, or surface-level analysis is a losing game. Instead, the future of consulting lies upstream, in territory that machines can't authentically occupy (yet):

Interpreting AI outputs within human systems: Factoring in political complexity, emotional stakes, and ethical trade-offs that algorithms can't fully grasp.

Guiding conversations that machines can't moderate: Leading leadership teams through difficult choices, conflicting values, and divergent visions that require human facilitation.

Serving as moral and strategic mirrors: Not offering definitive answers, but helping decision-makers ask deeper, more transformative questions that challenge assumptions and reveal blind spots.

The consultant who thrives in the AI age won't be the one with the fastest analysis. It will be the one who can hold space for complexity, translate between technical possibility and human reality, and help organizations make choices that serve not just metrics, but meaning.

Lawyers and Legal Strategists: The Shifting Value of Advocacy

Lawyers have long stood as pillars of logic, argument, and advocacy, guiding individuals, businesses, and societies through conflict, ambiguity, and governance. But in the age of AI, the foundations of legal work are being rapidly redefined.

AI systems can now analyze thousands of legal documents in seconds, identify precedents, flag inconsistencies, and even draft preliminary contracts or legal briefs. The utility is staggering and growing by the day. Law firms already use AI to automate research, due diligence, and predictive analytics, drastically cutting down time and costs.

And with platforms delivering algorithmic legal insights at scale, the perception of machine-generated legal input is improving. For standardized contracts, low-risk litigation, or compliance reviews, clients may begin to trust AI's efficiency more than a junior associate's painstaking hours. While writing this book, I built an AI-based application, burokratie.com, which actively assists users in navigating complex administrative and bureaucratic processes. The platform drafts structured, legally grounded responses to official correspondence, helps users understand their procedural options, and reduces the friction and uncertainty that typically accompany interactions with public administrations. The project demonstrates how legal reasoning and advocacy are beginning to shift from bespoke professional services toward scalable, productized systems.

When it comes to impact, AI-driven legal tools can increase access to justice by lowering barriers to legal services. In some cases, they may even outperform humans by reducing bias, increasing consistency, and improving efficiency in bureaucratic processes.

But Why Do We Still Hire Human Lawyers?

Despite all this, many people still seek out human lawyers, especially for high-stakes cases, complex disputes, or situations requiring deep strategic thinking. Because law is not only about rules, it's about interpretation, representation, and narrative.

However, this overlooks a critical reality: human lawyers have never been universally accessible.

For many people, immigrants, low-income individuals, those facing language barriers, or anyone outside the networks of power and privilege, quality legal representation has been either unaffordable or unavailable. A consultation that costs hundreds of euros per hour. Retainers that require thousands upfront. Lawyers who don't return calls or who dismiss cases they find unprofitable.

I experienced this personally in Germany. As someone with an immigration background, I faced a legal system where even understanding a court letter felt insurmountable. The thought of hiring a lawyer was not just expensive, it felt risky. Would they truly advocate for me? Would cultural or linguistic barriers undermine my case? The asymmetry was terrifying: anyone could sue me for anything, and I lacked the resources or connections to respond effectively.

When AI legal tools became available, they didn't replace my lawyer. They gave me access I never had. For the first time, I could understand legal documents, research my rights, and draft responses that were coherent and grounded in law. AI didn't take away human jobs from me. It provided a service I couldn't afford and probably wouldn't have received fairly anyway.

This reveals an uncomfortable truth: for millions of people worldwide, AI legal assistance isn't a threat to justice, it's an expansion of it.

Two Perspectives on AI in Law

This creates a paradox. For those who've had access to excellent legal representation, AI might seem like a downgrade, a loss of the human touch, empathy, and strategic brilliance a skilled lawyer provides.

But for those who've been locked out of that system, AI represents liberation. It's the difference between navigating a legal system blind and afraid, versus having some ability to understand and respond.

Both perspectives are valid, and both must inform how we think about value in legal services:

For those with access: The human lawyer's value lies in their ability to provide strategic wisdom, emotional support, and advocacy that goes beyond algorithmic analysis. They want someone who can stand in the gap during high-stakes decisions or life-altering disputes.

For those without access: AI provides baseline competence, language translation, document interpretation, and guidance that was previously unavailable at any price they could afford. The impact on their lives is profoundly positive.

The challenge for the legal profession isn't simply *"how do we compete with AI?"* It's *"how do we ensure that as AI democratizes access to basic legal services, we preserve and expand the distinctly human elements of justice for everyone, not just the privileged few?"*

The Evolution of Legal Value

In this changing landscape, the human lawyer who wants to remain valuable must acknowledge both realities. For high-value clients, that means moving away from merely processing law and leaning into embodying justice:

Interpreting AI-generated legal insights through the lens of human consequence. Understanding how a strategy may affect a person's dignity, safety, or future, not just their legal position.

Advocating in morally complex or emotionally charged environments. Where the nuances of tone, trauma, and cultural context matter as much as precedent and statute.

Crafting narratives, not just arguments. Because great lawyering isn't just about winning, it's about telling the truth in a way that moves hearts and minds.

But there's also a different path: expanding access. Lawyers who embrace AI as a tool to serve more people at lower costs, who focus on the cases that AI can't handle well, who provide affordable oversight and judgment on top of AI-generated work. This model serves justice more broadly while maintaining the essential human role in the legal system.

The lawyer of tomorrow must become less of a gatekeeper and more of a bridge, connecting people to justice whether through their own direct service or through AI-augmented tools they help clients navigate. Between code and community. Between regulation and reality. Between what the law says and what justice requires for all people, not just those who can afford premium representation.

Doctors and Healthcare Professionals: Healing in the Age of Intelligent Systems

Medicine is one of humanity's most sacred professions, rooted in trust, knowledge, and compassion. For centuries, doctors have been stewards of life and wellness, diagnosing illness, relieving suffering, and walking with patients through some of life's most vulnerable moments.

But today, AI is reshaping the landscape of healthcare with breathtaking speed. Modern systems can now analyze radiology scans faster and more accurately than trained specialists, predict disease risk based on genetic data, and optimize treatment plans using machine learning models. The utility of AI in medicine is transformative, enhancing diagnostic precision, reducing human error, and increasing the efficiency of clinical workflows.

The perception of AI in healthcare is also evolving. Many patients and providers now trust AI-driven tools for early screening, remote monitoring, and chronic disease management. In some areas, people even prefer AI-driven triage systems for their speed and consistency over overworked human clinics.

And when it comes to impact, AI has already saved lives. It enables earlier diagnoses, more personalized care plans, and improved access in underserved regions through telemedicine and mobile diagnostics.

Why Do Patients Still Want Human Doctors?

Despite this rising dominance, most patients still want a human in the room when it comes to their actual care. Why? Because health is not just a technical condition, it's a deeply emotional, existential, and relational experience. Patients aren't only looking for answers. They are often looking for understanding, presence, and hope.

Human doctors bring perceived value through their capacity to empathize, reassure, and hold space for complexity. A patient doesn't just want to know what the treatment is. They want to feel that someone truly cares whether they live or die.

But there's another dimension to healthcare that's less visible and often more frustrating: the bureaucratic maze that surrounds medical care.

The Hidden Healthcare Crisis: Navigating the System

In Germany, where I live, health insurance is mandatory. This sounds straightforward until you try to navigate it as someone whose life doesn't fit the standard template. As a consultant who travels the world and spends most of my time abroad, finding the right coverage that would protect me during my international movements became a nightmare.

I found myself trapped with an insurer whose bureaucratic demands became absurd. Every month, they sent forms requiring me to report income changes so they could adjust premiums accordingly. I would return from international travel, exhausted, and the first thing awaiting me was another form to fill out. Miss the deadline, and they would raise the premium to the maximum at their sole discretion.

Then it got worse. Without informing me clearly, they started charging an additional penalty for non-response every three days. At Christmas, I received a letter stating I owed approximately 15,000 euros in missed premiums and penalties for having failed to comply with their bureaucratic process.

I felt helpless. The system was designed in a way that assumed everyone had a stable, predictable life with regular income and plenty of time to manage paperwork. For someone like me, it was a trap. And I knew I wasn't alone. Millions of people worldwide face similar situations where healthcare systems, designed to help, become sources of stress and financial vulnerability.

This is where AI changed everything for me.

Using AI legal and regulatory tools, I was able to research German insurance law and discovered something crucial: according to German regulations, one cannot be required to pay for two health insurance policies simultaneously. I had maintained coverage abroad during my travels, which meant the German insurer's demands were legally questionable.

Armed with this knowledge, I could build a case. The AI didn't just give me information, it gave me power in a situation where I had felt utterly powerless. It translated complex legal language into something I could understand and use. It helped me navigate a system that was designed to be impenetrable for someone in my position.

That insurer tried every means to extract the money from me, but that's a story for another book. The point is this: AI didn't replace human healthcare professionals in my life. It protected me from a dehumanizing system that human bureaucrats had created and maintained.

Two Faces of Healthcare AI

This experience reveals that AI in healthcare isn't just about diagnosis and treatment. It's also about access, navigation, and protection. There are two distinct ways AI creates value in healthcare:

Clinical AI: Improving diagnosis, treatment planning, and medical outcomes. This is where the conversation about AI versus human doctors usually focuses.

Systemic AI: Helping patients navigate insurance, understand their rights, decode medical bills, and fight bureaucratic injustice. This is equally important but less discussed.

For clinical care, most people still prefer human doctors for the reasons we've discussed: empathy, presence, holistic understanding. But for navigating healthcare systems, many people would gladly choose AI over the faceless bureaucracy that currently governs access to care.

The Doctor as Guardian of Meaning

In this fast-shifting ecosystem, doctors must reimagine their roles, not just as providers of care, but as guardians of meaning in the healing process. That means:

Interpreting AI-generated data in the context of human complexity. Understanding not just what the data says, but how it aligns with a patient's values, fears, and life goals. A treatment that maximizes survival time might not be the right choice for a patient who prioritizes quality of life over quantity.

Navigating moral ambiguity. When life, death, and suffering don't fit into a formula, and ethical decisions require courage, not code. When families disagree about treatment. When resources are limited, and choices must be made about who receives care.

Providing spiritual and emotional presence. Especially when medicine reaches its limits and healing becomes about acceptance, dignity, and closure. When the work is no longer about curing disease but about accompanying someone through their final chapter with compassion and grace.

Advocating for patients within broken systems. Standing between vulnerable patients and bureaucratic machinery that treats them as numbers rather than human beings. Sometimes the most important thing a doctor can do isn't prescribe medication, but help a patient fight an insurance denial or navigate administrative barriers to care.

The physician who thrives in the AI age won't be the one who can read scans fastest. It will be the one who can sit with suffering, honor the whole person, help patients make decisions that honor their lives, and fight for their access to care when systems fail them.

And perhaps, as AI tools become more sophisticated at helping patients navigate bureaucratic mazes, doctors can spend less time on paperwork and more time on what only humans can do: being fully present with another human being in their most vulnerable moments.

Politicians and Public Leaders:

Politics has always been about representation, vision, and the art of balancing competing interests in the service of the public good. Traditionally, we've entrusted this role to human beings because we believed that only a human could embody our stories, our struggles, and our soul.

But artificial intelligence is now pressing against the very doors of governance.

Governments around the world are already using AI to monitor dissent and social unrest, allocate public resources with algorithmic precision, and manage traffic, urban infrastructure, and even elements of public health and safety. These tasks, once reserved for technocrats, are now increasingly managed by data-driven systems.

The Utility Question

Utility: AI can model economic scenarios, generate optimized public policies, and coordinate disaster response systems faster and more accurately than any human bureaucracy. It doesn't fatigue, doesn't require sleep, and isn't swayed by ego or partisanship. In terms of pure administrative efficiency, AI could theoretically govern better than most human leaders.

But the deeper question isn't whether AI can manage a country. It's whether AI can represent one. Leadership isn't just about delivering efficient outcomes, it's about making hard choices that reflect a nation's soul. It's about knowing when to act against what's optimal in favor of what's right. It's about walking with people through pain, hope, and transformation.

For now, humans still lead because we still want our leaders to be mortal, fallible, and emotionally alive, a mirror to our humanity. But if AI evolves to convincingly simulate all that, would we notice, or care?

The Perception Challenge

Perception: This is where resistance still lives. While some citizens welcome efficiency, many are wary of surrendering political power to machines. AI may lack the perceived ability to understand suffering, to forgive, to inspire, traits we associate with real leadership.

We want leaders who have experienced loss, who have struggled with difficult choices, who carry the weight of their decisions. We want leaders who can be moved by a child's tears or an elder's wisdom. Can an algorithm truly understand what it means to lead a people through crisis, to ask them for sacrifice, to offer them hope when the future is uncertain?

The Impact Dilemma

Impact: AI-led governance could bring unprecedented system-wide efficiency and fairness, eliminating human bias, reducing corruption, and accelerating implementation. Imagine policies optimized purely for the greatest good, untainted by special interests or political calculations.

But it could also erode the moral and emotional dimensions of leadership: the capacity for grace, sacrifice, and bold ethical stands. History's greatest leaders, from Lincoln to Mandela, were great not because they optimized outcomes, but because they embodied values and inspired transformation. They made choices that the data didn't support but that their moral compass demanded.

Would an AI have freed the slaves when it was economically disruptive? Would it have pursued reconciliation when punishment was more efficient? Would it risk political capital to protect vulnerable minorities when the majority demands otherwise?

Citizenship for Robots: A Sign of What's Coming?

When Saudi Arabia granted citizenship to a humanoid robot named Sophia in 2017, it sparked global debate. Some laughed. Others worried. But many asked a deeper question: If a robot can be a citizen, what stops it from becoming a political candidate?

And indeed, if AI-driven humanoids fulfill legal eligibility requirements (residency, age, etc.), demonstrate communication skills, charisma, and fluency in human emotions, and are backed by voters (or algorithms deciding for them), then electing a machine to high office may no longer be the realm of science fiction.

Will we elect a humanoid president one day? Perhaps the question isn't if, but when, and what we'll lose or gain in the process.

Summary: The Three Dimensions Across Professions

The table below summarizes how AI is reshaping value across the professions we've explored, viewed through the three dimensions of value: utility, perception, and impact

Profession	Utility	Perception	Impact
Consultants & Strategic Advisors	High and accelerating. AI analyzes data faster, models scenarios with precision, and generates evidence-based recommendations at scale.	Shifting toward AI. As algorithmic outputs become more sophisticated and personalized, clients increasingly trust machine-generated insights, especially for cost and speed.	Mixed. AI can prevent financial losses and optimize systems efficiently. But human consultants navigate political complexity, emotional stakes, and ethical trade-offs that algorithms miss.
Lawyers & Legal Strategists	Very high. AI conducts legal research, analyzes documents, identifies precedents, and drafts contracts in seconds. For routine legal work, AI utility is transformative.	Improving for routine work. Clients trust AI for standardized contracts and compliance. But for complex cases, human lawyers retain perceived value through empathy, advocacy, and strategic wisdom. Critical note: For marginalized groups, AI provides access to legal understanding previously unavailable.	Democratizing access. AI expands legal services to those who couldn't afford lawyers. But human lawyers remain essential for morally complex cases and crafting narratives that move hearts.

Profession	Utility	Perception	Impact
Doctors & Healthcare Professionals	Transformative in diagnostics. AI analyzes scans faster and more accurately than specialists, predicts disease risk, and optimizes treatment plans. Also crucial systemically: AI helps patients navigate insurance bureaucracy and decode complex regulations.	Growing for diagnostics, resistant for care. Patients trust AI tools for screening and monitoring but still prefer human doctors for diagnosis, treatment decisions, and emotional support during vulnerability.	Life-saving clinically. Enables earlier diagnosis and personalized care. Protective systemically: Helps patients fight bureaucratic injustice and access their rights. Human presence remains irreplaceable in end-of-life care and moral decision-making.
Politicians & Public Leaders	Potentially superior. AI can model policies, allocate resources optimally, and coordinate systems without fatigue, ego, or corruption. Governance efficiency could surpass human capacity.	Strong resistance. Most citizens want leaders who are mortal, emotionally alive, and can embody their struggles. AI lacks perceived ability to understand suffering, forgive, or inspire through shared humanity.	Uncertain and profound. Could eliminate bias and corruption, but might erode moral leadership, grace, and the capacity for bold ethical stands that defy optimization.

Key Insights from the Framework

Looking across these professions, several patterns emerge:

1. **Utility is AI's strongest dimension**: Across every profession, AI delivers measurable efficiency gains, speed, and analytical power that humans cannot match.

2. **Perception is the battleground.**:Public trust in AI varies dramatically by context. Routine tasks see growing acceptance; high-stakes, emotionally charged situations retain preference for humans.

3. **Impact reveals the deepest questions**: AI's long-term consequences—social, ethical, existential—remain uncertain and demand human wisdom to navigate.

4. **Access and equity matter**: For privileged individuals with resources, AI may seem like a downgrade from premium human services. For those historically excluded from quality services (legal representation, healthcare navigation), AI represents unprecedented access and empowerment.

5. **The human opportunity lies upstream**: Competing with AI on speed and scale is futile. The future belongs to those who focus on what machines cannot do, navigate moral complexity, build trust through presence, craft meaning from data, and advocate for justice beyond mere efficiency.

As we move into Chapter 3, we'll explore the great shift this creates: from valuing efficiency above all else to recognizing that in an AI-abundant world, meaning, ethics, and genuine human service become the new premium.

After Efficiency

Chapter 3

The Great Shift:
From Efficiency to Meaning

How AI Disrupts Traditional Value Systems

For over a century, our economic and social systems have been anchored in the pursuit of efficiency. The industrial revolution celebrated mechanization. The digital age lauded automation. Productivity became synonymous with progress, and human worth was often measured by output.

Enter artificial intelligence, a force that doesn't just enhance efficiency but redefines it. AI systems now outperform humans in data analysis, pattern recognition, and even creative endeavors like composing music or drafting articles. Tasks once deemed uniquely human are now executed faster and, in some cases, more accurately by machines.

This evolution challenges our traditional value systems. If machines can replicate or surpass human capabilities in various domains, what distinguishes human contribution? The metrics of success are shifting, prompting a reevaluation of what we truly value in work and society.

The shift is profound because efficiency itself has become abundant. When everyone can access tools that deliver speed and scale, efficiency ceases to be a differentiator. It becomes table stakes. The new scarcity, and therefore the new premium, lies elsewhere: in meaning, purpose, judgment, and the distinctly human capacities that machines cannot replicate.

Why Productivity Is No Longer Enough

In the age of AI, raw productivity is abundant. Algorithms can churn out content, optimize logistics, and manage financial portfolios with unprecedented speed. However, this surge in efficiency brings forth a paradox: as machines handle more tasks, the human role becomes less about doing and more about deciding.

Productivity, once the pinnacle of achievement, is now a baseline expectation. The differentiators are no longer how much we produce but how we infuse our work with purpose, ethics, and emotional intelligence. The question isn't just *"Can it be done?"* but *"Should it be done?"* and *"Who does it serve?"*

I've experienced this shift personally in my consulting work. I now sometimes use AI to brainstorm and generate additional ideas, which I then confront with my own experience and judgment. The AI might suggest approaches I hadn't immediately thought of, opening different paths for exploration. Combined with my two decades of experience in climate finance and international development, I can create consulting products today that are more complete, more thoroughly researched, and more nuanced than I could have produced alone, and with fewer resources.

But here's where it gets tricky, and where the difference between productivity and value becomes crystal clear.

The Illusion of Productivity: A Cautionary Tale

Last year, I hired a young professional to assist me in drafting a concept note for one of my clients. I gave her the background, explained the client's context, and asked her to develop an initial draft we could refine together.

When she submitted her work, I was distressed. She had used AI to generate the entire paper. It was polished, professional-looking, and utterly generic. It missed the crux of what the client wanted. There was no value added or created by her work. It was productivity without purpose, output without insight.

The paper used all the right buzzwords but lacked any real understanding of the client's unique situation. It could have been written for any organization, in any sector, addressing any problem. The AI had optimized for coherence and structure but had no way to know that when this particular client used the term *"community engagement,"* they meant something very specific, shaped by a failed project three years earlier that had left lasting distrust.

We sat down together, and I walked her through the document. I showed her patterns in how this client communicated, words that carried specific meanings in their organizational culture, unstated assumptions that shaped their decision-making. I explained how my experience with similar clients in similar contexts informed my interpretation of what they were really asking for beneath the surface request.

The AI had produced a document. But it hadn't created value. Creating value required understanding context, reading between the lines, and bringing judgment informed by experience. It required knowing not just what to say, but the problem this particular client needed to solve, in this particular moment, given their particular history and constraints.

This experience crystallized something important: AI makes it easier than ever to be productive. But it also makes it easier than ever to generate work that looks valuable but isn't. The gap between output and impact can be invisible to those who confuse activity with contribution.

The Growing Premium on Human-Centered Value

As AI takes over routine tasks, human-centered qualities gain prominence. Three capacities in particular are becoming the new differentiators:

Creativity: Vision Beyond Patterns

While AI can generate content based on existing data, genuine creativity involves original thought, risk-taking, and the ability to connect disparate ideas in novel ways. Human creativity is driven by experiences, emotions, and cultural contexts that machines cannot fully comprehend.

AI can show you variations within known spaces. It can interpolate between existing solutions. But it cannot make the intuitive leap to an entirely new paradigm. It cannot look at a problem and say, *"What if we've been asking the wrong question this whole time?"*

When I use AI for brainstorming, it's most valuable not when it gives me answers, but when it helps me explore adjacent possibilities that trigger my own creative insights. The AI maps the terrain. I decide where to build.

Ethics: Judgment in Gray Areas

As we discussed in Chapter 1, impact is one of the three dimensions of value. And impact inevitably involves ethical considerations: Who benefits? Who bears the costs? What are the second-order effects? What values are we serving or compromising?

AI can be programmed to follow ethical rules, but it cannot engage in genuine ethical reasoning when faced with novel dilemmas where principles conflict. When efficiency and equity pull in opposite directions, AI optimizes for whichever objective it was given. Humans wrestle with which objective should take priority and why.

Empathy: Connection in an Age of Simulation

Empathy, the ability to genuinely understand and share the feelings of another, is becoming more valuable precisely because it's becoming rarer. In a world of AI-generated responses and automated interactions, genuine human presence and care stand out.

Empathy isn't just a soft skill. It's a strategic advantage. It allows you to understand what people actually need versus what they think they need or what they're asking for. It enables you to build trust in ways that no algorithm can replicate. It makes you irreplaceable.

AI and the Value Equation: Capabilities and Constraints

To navigate the future of value creation, we must first understand AI's true capabilities and limitations. The popular narrative often swings between two extremes: AI as either our savior or our replacement. The reality is more nuanced.

What AI Excels At

AI thrives in environments where success can be measured, patterns can be identified, and outcomes can be optimized.

- **Pattern Recognition at Scale**: AI can analyze millions of data points to identify trends invisible to human observation. In medical imaging, AI systems can detect early-stage cancers by recognizing subtle patterns across thousands of scans that even experienced radiologists might miss.

- **Optimization Under Constraints**: When variables are known and goals are clear, AI can find optimal solutions faster than any human team. Supply chain management, route optimization, and resource allocation are domains where AI demonstrably outperforms human decision-making in both speed and accuracy.

- **Consistency and Endurance**: Unlike humans, AI doesn't tire, doesn't have bad days, and doesn't bring personal biases into repetitive tasks. A customer service chatbot can maintain the same tone and accuracy at 3 AM as it does at 3 PM, serving customers across time zones without fatigue.

- **Rapid Iteration and Testing**: AI can run thousands of simulations in hours, testing scenarios that would take human teams months or years to evaluate. This allows for unprecedented experimentation and refinement.

What AI Struggles With

Despite its impressive capabilities, AI faces fundamental limitations:

- **Contextual Understanding**: AI lacks the lived experience that allows humans to understand nuance, read between lines, and grasp the unspoken weight of a situation. When a client says, *"We need this done quickly, but carefully,"* a human consultant understands the tension and priority hierarchy. AI sees contradictory instructions. This was precisely the problem with my junior colleague's AI-generated document. The AI had no way to understand that *"community engagement"* meant something very specific to this client based on their history. It couldn't read the subtext in the brief or anticipate the unspoken concerns that would shape how the document was received.

- **Ethical Reasoning in Novel Situations**: AI can be trained on ethical frameworks, but when faced with genuinely new moral dilemmas, situations without precedent, it cannot engage in the kind of philosophical reasoning that draws from human values, culture, and conscience. It cannot ask, *"Is this the right thing to do?"* in contexts where *"right"* hasn't been clearly defined.

- **Genuine Creativity**: While AI can remix, recombine, and interpolate existing patterns to generate *"novel"* outputs, it doesn't create from genuine inspiration, personal struggle, or transcendent insight. It produces variations. Humans produce visions. When I brainstorm with AI, it helps me explore the adjacent possible. But the breakthrough insights, the ideas that genuinely transform how we approach a problem, those still come from human intuition, experience, and the willingness to challenge assumptions.

- **Building Trust Through Presence**: Trust isn't just built through competence, it's built through vulnerability, commitment, and showing up consistently over time. AI can simulate reliability, but it cannot stake its reputation, feel shame, or demonstrate moral courage. It cannot be held accountable in the way a human can.

The New Roles of Data, Algorithms, and Human Oversight

In the AI-augmented economy, value creation increasingly depends on a trinity of forces working in concert: data, algorithms, and human judgment. Understanding how these three interact is essential for anyone seeking to create meaningful value.

Data: The Raw Material

Data is the fuel of AI systems, but not all data is created equal. The value equation begins with quality, context, and ethics.

- **Quality over Quantity**: More data doesn't always mean better outcomes. Clean, relevant, representative data trumps massive datasets riddled with bias or noise. A healthcare AI trained on diverse patient populations will outperform one trained on millions of records from a single demographic, no matter how large that dataset.

- **Context Preservation**: Data without context is just numbers. When organizations strip away the human stories, cultural nuances, and situational factors from their datasets, they create AI systems that optimize for metrics while missing meaning. This is why my colleague's AI-generated document failed. The AI had data about what a concept note should look like, but no context about what this particular client needed.

- **Ethical Sourcing**: As data becomes more valuable, questions of consent, ownership, and extraction become critical. Who owns the data? Who benefits from its use? These aren't just legal questions, they're value questions that shape whether we're creating systems that serve people or exploit them.

Algorithms: The Transformative Engine

Algorithms turn data into decisions, predictions, and recommendations. But their value depends on transparency, adaptability, and alignment.

- **Transparency**: Black-box algorithms that make consequential decisions without explanation erode trust. The future belongs to systems that can show their work, explain their reasoning, and allow for human intervention when needed.

- **Adaptability**: Static algorithms quickly become obsolete. The most valuable systems learn continuously, adjusting to changing conditions while maintaining core principles. But this adaptability must be guided, not unconstrained, which is where human oversight becomes essential.

- **Alignment**: An algorithm optimized for the wrong goal creates negative value, no matter how efficiently it operates. A social media algorithm optimized purely for engagement time may maximize addiction while destroying attention spans and mental health. Success isn't just achieving the goal you set. It's setting the right goal in the first place.

Human Oversight: The Ethical Governor

This is where human judgment becomes not just valuable but irreplaceable.

Setting the Objective Function: Humans must define what *"success"* means, not just in measurable terms, but in moral ones. Should the algorithm prioritize efficiency or equity? Short-term gains or long-term sustainability? Maximum output or sustainable wellbeing? These aren't technical questions. They're value questions that require human judgment.

Interpreting Edge Cases: When AI encounters situations outside its training data, human judgment fills the gap. A loan algorithm might flag an applicant based on data patterns, but a human loan officer can recognize that the applicant is a refugee with no local credit history but strong prospects and solid character references. The algorithm sees risk. The human sees potential.

Accepting Responsibility: When things go wrong, and they will, humans must bear accountability. This isn't a burden to avoid but a source of authority to embrace. The willingness to be held responsible is what separates leaders from tools. AI can optimize, but humans must answer for the outcomes.

Case Studies: Value Creation in AI-Rich Sectors

Let's examine how the interplay of AI and human judgment is reshaping value creation in three critical sectors. Each case study illustrates how the three dimensions of value (perception, utility, and impact) manifest in practice.

Healthcare: Diagnosis Meets Discernment

The AI Revolution:

At Duke University, an AI system analyzes sepsis risk in real-time, monitoring patient vitals and alerting doctors hours before traditional methods would catch the warning signs. The system processes thousands of data points per second, catching subtle patterns that could save lives. The utility is extraordinary.

The Human Element:

But here's what the AI can't do: When it flags a patient, a human physician must decide whether to initiate aggressive treatment, which carries its own risks, or continue monitoring. This decision requires not just clinical knowledge but understanding the patient's values, their quality of life considerations, and their family's capacity to cope with different outcomes.

Dr. Sarah Chen, an ICU physician working with the system, explains: *"The AI gives me superhuman awareness. But I give the AI something it can't have: the ability to sit with a patient's daughter and help her understand that sometimes the most compassionate choice isn't the most aggressive one."*

Value Created:

The combination achieves something neither could alone. Earlier intervention with fewer false alarms and treatment decisions that honor both clinical best practices and human dignity. Patient outcomes improve by 18% (strong impact), but equally important, families report feeling more supported through difficult decisions (strong perception). The AI delivers utility. The human delivers meaning.

Finance: Algorithms Meet Accountability

The AI Revolution:

Hedge funds now use AI to execute trades in microseconds, analyzing news sentiment, market patterns, and global events simultaneously. Some algorithms manage billions without human intervention for days at a time. The utility for speed and pattern recognition is unmatched.

The Human Element:

Yet the most successful firms maintain a crucial constraint: humans set the risk parameters and can override any trade. When an algorithm recommended massive short positions on Italian bonds in 2022 based purely on data patterns, human traders recognized something the AI couldn't: the political will to prevent a European debt crisis was far stronger than historical patterns suggested.

James Morrison, CIO of a major investment firm, notes:

"Our AI is smarter than any individual trader. But our human team is wiser than our AI. Wisdom isn't just about predicting outcomes. It's about understanding which outcomes are tolerable and which would destroy trust in the system we depend on."

Value Created:

The hybrid approach generates returns that beat pure AI systems in volatile markets while maintaining risk profiles that allow clients to sleep at night. More importantly, when markets panic, human judgment prevents the kind of algorithmic cascade failures that can turn market corrections into crashes. The impact isn't just on returns, but on systemic stability. And the perception among clients is that their money is managed not just intelligently, but responsibly.

Art and Creative Industries: Generation Meets Soul

The AI Revolution:

AI can now generate images, music, and written content that is technically impressive and commercially viable. Stock photography sites are flooded with AI-generated images. Advertising agencies use AI to produce dozens of campaign variations in hours. The utility for rapid content creation is undeniable.

The Human Element:

Yet the pieces that truly move people, that go viral, that win awards, that get remembered, almost always involve deep human curation, direction, and vision. AI is a tool in the hands of artists, not a replacement for artistic vision.

Yuki Tanaka, a visual artist who incorporates AI into her work, explains her process:

"I use AI to generate hundreds of variations, but I'm not looking for the 'best' one by any algorithmic measure. I'm looking for the one that speaks to something true about the human experience I'm trying to capture. The AI can show me possibilities I wouldn't have imagined, but only I can recognize which one has soul."

Value Created:

The combination allows for unprecedented creative experimentation while maintaining the essential human quality that makes art meaningful. Tanaka's work sells for premium prices not despite using AI, but because she's found a way to use it that amplifies rather than replaces human insight.

Looking through our three dimensions: The utility is high (AI generates hundreds of variations quickly, Tanaka curates with expert judgment). The perception is strong (collectors believe they're buying human creativity augmented by technology, not technology masquerading as creativity). And the impact is profound (art that genuinely moves people rather than merely impressive technical demonstrations). All three dimensions align, creating sustainable value that commands premium pricing.

The Emerging Pattern: Augmentation, Not Replacement

Across these sectors, a consistent pattern emerges: maximum value is created not when AI replaces humans or when humans ignore AI, but when the two work in complementary roles.

The Integrated Value Equation

Value = [(AI Utility × Human Judgment) × Perception] + Impact

Where:

AI Utility: The functional capability AI brings (speed, scale, pattern recognition, consistency, tireless optimization)

Human Judgment: The contextual wisdom, ethical reasoning, creative vision, and accountability that humans provide (context, meaning, interpretation, responsibility)

Perception: How stakeholders view and trust the combined human-AI output (authenticity, trustworthiness, legitimacy)

Impact: The broader consequences (social, environmental, economic) that emerge from ethical alignment and responsible deployment

Understanding the Mathematics of Value

The multiplication between AI Utility and Human Judgment reflects a critical truth: when either is zero, no value is created. An AI without human oversight can optimize toward harmful outcomes. A human without AI augmentation increasingly can't compete on efficiency, reach, or scale. But when both work together, utility multiplies beyond what either could achieve alone.

This is precisely what happened with my junior colleague. She had AI utility but applied zero human judgment. Zero multiplied by anything equals zero. Despite the appearance of productivity, she created no value.

Their product is then multiplied by Perception, because even excellent work has limited value if stakeholders don't trust or recognize it. You can have brilliant AI capability and sound human judgment, but if people don't perceive your work as trustworthy, authentic, or legitimate, its value is severely limited.

Finally, Impact is added as the dimension that determines whether value is sustainable and serves human flourishing. This sits somewhat separately because ethical impact can exist independent of utility and perception. A project might have low utility and weak perception but still create positive impact through its ethical commitments. Conversely, high utility and strong perception don't guarantee positive impact if the work isn't ethically aligned.

This equation explains why:

- **The Duke sepsis AI creates value**: High AI utility (pattern recognition) multiplied by high human judgment (treatment decisions considering patient values) multiplied by strong perception (families trust the process) plus positive impact (lives saved with dignity honored).

- **The hedge fund AI creates value**: High AI utility (trade execution) multiplied by human judgment (risk parameters and overrides) multiplied by strong perception (client trust) plus positive impact (market stability preserved).

- **Tanaka's AI art creates value**: High AI utility (variation generation) multiplied by human judgment (curation with soul) multiplied by strong perception (collectors value human creativity) plus positive impact (art that moves people).

- **My consulting work creates value**: AI utility (brainstorming and analysis) multiplied by my professional judgment (two decades of experience) multiplied by client perception (both efficient and deeply informed) plus positive impact (solutions that serve genuine needs).

In each case, all elements of the equation must be present and positive for maximum value creation. Remove any one element, and value diminishes or disappears entirely.

Moving Forward: From Understanding to Action

As we transition to Part II of this book, we'll explore how to cultivate the uniquely human capacities that make you irreplaceable in the AI age. Because understanding what AI can do is only half the equation. The other half is understanding what only you can offer and learning to lead with that.

The great shift from efficiency to meaning isn't just philosophical. It's practical and urgent. In a world where productivity is abundant, the professionals, organizations, and societies that thrive will be those that learn to create value through wisdom, judgment, ethics, and genuine human service.

The question isn't whether AI will change your profession. It will. The question is whether you'll use this change as an opportunity to become more human, more purposeful, and more valuable, or whether you'll try to compete with machines on their terms and lose.

The choice is yours. But the path forward is clear: embrace AI for what it does well, develop yourself for what only you can do, and never confuse output with impact, productivity with value, or efficiency with meaning.

PART II
Rethinking Human Worth
and Contribution

Chapter 4

The Human Dividend

In a world where machines can increasingly replicate cognitive tasks, a paradox emerges: the more AI can do, the more valuable certain human qualities become. This isn't wishful thinking or romantic nostalgia. It's economic reality driven by scarcity, trust, and the fundamental nature of what people actually want.

We're witnessing the emergence of what I call the Human Dividend, the premium value that accrues to those who develop and deploy uniquely human capacities in an AI-saturated world.

What Uniquely Human Traits Are Becoming More Valuable

As AI commoditizes technical skills and knowledge work, several human capacities are emerging as the new sources of competitive advantage. Looking through our three dimensions of value, these capacities score exceptionally high on perception and impact, even when their immediate utility might seem less quantifiable than AI's capabilities.>

Emotional Intelligence: Reading What Isn't Said

Emotional intelligence, the ability to recognize, understand, and respond to emotions in yourself and others, is proving to be one of the most valuable human traits in the AI age.

Consider the work of a therapist. An AI chatbot can be trained on every therapy technique, can recall every session perfectly, and can operate 24/7 at minimal cost. Some therapy bots are already in use and show promising results for specific conditions.

Yet most people, when facing a genuine crisis, still seek a human therapist. Why?

Because healing doesn't happen through perfect technique. It happens through connection. A human therapist notices when your voice changes as you discuss your mother. They catch the pause before you answer a question about your marriage. They feel the weight in the room when you're not saying what you really need to say.

Dr. Michael Torres, a clinical psychologist, describes it this way: *"My clients don't come to me because I know more than an AI about cognitive behavioral therapy. The AI probably knows more. They come because when they cry, I feel something too. And they know I feel it. That mutual vulnerability, that's where transformation happens."*

This principle extends far beyond therapy. In leadership, the best leaders don't just make optimal decisions. They understand how those decisions will land emotionally with their teams and adjust accordingly. In sales, top performers don't just solve problems. They sense what the client is afraid to say and create safety for honest conversation. In teaching, master educators don't just transfer information. They read their students' confusion, frustration, and breakthroughs in real time and adapt.

The utility of emotional intelligence might seem soft compared to AI's hard metrics, but its perception value is extraordinarily high (people deeply trust those who understand them emotionally), and its impact is profound (it creates transformation, loyalty, and sustainable relationships that algorithms cannot replicate).

Storytelling: Meaning-Making in an Information-Saturated World

AI can generate text. It can even generate narratives. But storytelling, the ancient human art of packaging truth in a form that moves hearts and changes minds, remains distinctly human.

The difference is this: AI can tell you what happened. Humans tell you what it meant.

Sarah Martinez built a successful sustainability consulting firm not by having better data than her competitors. Several had access to the same climate models and impact metrics. She won clients by telling stories that made climate action feel urgent and achievable rather than overwhelming and futile.

"I worked with a manufacturing CEO who was drowning in sustainability reports," Sarah recalls. *"He had all the data, but it wasn't moving him to action. So I stopped showing him charts and instead told him about the factory worker I met who showed me pictures of his grandchildren and asked if they'd be able to live in his hometown in 50 years. Suddenly, carbon reduction wasn't an abstract metric. It was about whether this man's grandchildren would have water to drink."*

That's storytelling: finding the human truth in the data and sharing it in a way that creates connection and compels action.

In business, this skill is increasingly valuable. In marketing, as consumers are bombarded with AI-generated content, the stories that break through are those with genuine human struggle, transformation, and triumph. In change management, organizations don't transform because of PowerPoint decks. They transform because leaders tell compelling stories about where they're going and why it matters. In fundraising, investors don't fund spreadsheets. They fund visions wrapped in narratives they can believe in.

Judgment: Navigating Ambiguity and Moral Complexity

Perhaps no human capacity is more valuable, and less replicable by AI, than judgment: the ability to make sound decisions when information is incomplete, stakes are high, and there's no clear *"right"* answer.

Judgment isn't just intelligence. It's wisdom, the synthesis of experience, values, intuition, and careful reasoning applied to situations where the usual rules don't quite fit.

Consider a hospital administrator deciding whether to invest in expensive equipment that could save lives but might bankrupt the institution. The AI can model financial outcomes and patient impact, but it can't decide how much financial risk is appropriate to take to save how many potential lives. That's a judgment call, one that requires weighing competing goods against each other.

Or consider a journalist deciding whether to publish a story that's technically accurate but could ruin someone's life. The facts can be verified, the sources checked. But should it be published? That requires judgment about public interest, proportionality, and human dignity, things that can't be reduced to algorithm.

Marcus Chen, a venture capital partner, describes his work this way: *"Our AI can predict with 87% accuracy whether a startup's metrics will hit their targets. But it can't tell me whether the founder has the character to navigate the inevitable crisis that will come. It can't assess whether they'll be honest when things go wrong or whether they'll throw their team under the bus. Those judgment calls separate investments that return 3x from those that return 30x."*

Trust: The Ultimate Scarcity in an Age of Simulation

As AI-generated content becomes increasingly sophisticated and indistinguishable from human creation, trust becomes the scarcest and most valuable commodity.

Trust isn't just about competence. It's about knowing that someone will do the right thing even when no one is watching, even when it costs them something, even when the algorithm would recommend otherwise.

This is why, despite the efficiency of automated systems, people still value personal recommendations over algorithmic suggestions, handwritten notes over templated emails, face-to-face meetings over video calls, and long-term relationships over transactional interactions.

The human capacity to build trust through consistency, vulnerability, and demonstrated care is becoming a source of tremendous value. In a world where you can't be sure if you're interacting with a person or a bot, the people and organizations that prove their humanity command a premium.

Through our value dimensions: Trust has moderate utility (it takes time to build), but extraordinarily high perception (people prefer dealing with those they trust even at higher cost or lower efficiency), and its impact is foundational (trust enables all other forms of value creation and collaboration).

The Four Pillars of Human Value

These four capacities (emotional intelligence, storytelling, judgment, and trust) aren't separate skills but interconnected dimensions of human capability. Together, they form what we might call the Human Dividend.

The good news: unlike technical skills that can be learned from a textbook or tutorial, these capacities are developed through lived experience, relationships, and reflection. They're resistant to commoditization precisely because they emerge from the unrepeatable specificity of each person's life.

The challenge: most of our educational and professional systems were built to develop technical and analytical skills, not these deeper human capacities. Cultivating the Human Dividend requires intentional practice and often means unlearning habits of optimization and efficiency in favor of presence, connection, and wisdom.

AI as Augmentation, Not Replacement

Understanding the Human Dividend leads to a crucial realization: the future isn't about humans versus AI. It's about humans with AI versus humans without AI.

The professionals who will thrive aren't those who reject AI or those who blindly embrace it, but those who learn to use AI to augment their uniquely human capabilities.

The Augmentation Mindset in Practice

Dr. Jennifer Walsh, a family physician, describes her evolving practice:

"When AI diagnostic tools first appeared, I was threatened. Was I going to be replaced by an algorithm? Then I realized the AI could review symptoms, flag patterns, and suggest diagnoses faster than I ever could. That freed me to spend time actually talking to patients, understanding the context of their lives, asking about the stresses and relationships and habits that don't show up in their blood work but massively impact their health.

Now I'm a better doctor than I ever was. Not because I'm smarter, but because I let AI handle what it's good at so I can focus on what only I can do: being present with another human being who's suffering and helping them find a path to wellness that fits their actual life, not just their medical chart."

This is the augmentation mindset: using AI to handle the routine, the analytical, the pattern-recognition tasks so that you can focus your human energy on the irreplaceable work of connection, judgment, and meaning-making.

The Three Questions of Augmentation

To develop an augmentation mindset, ask yourself:

1. What can AI do better than me? (Let it do that)
2. What can I do better than AI? (Focus your energy there)
3. What can we do together that neither could do alone? (That's where the magic happens)

A graphic designer might answer: AI can generate hundreds of layout variations instantly. I can recognize which design will resonate with this specific client's brand identity and emotional goals. Together, we can explore creative possibilities I'd never have time to sketch and refine them with human judgment.

A financial advisor might answer: AI can optimize portfolio allocations and rebalance automatically. I can help clients stay committed to their strategy during market panics and make adjustments when their life circumstances change. Together, we can deliver both superior returns and the emotional support that prevents panic selling.

The Multiplication Effect

Here's the crucial insight: when you properly augment your human capabilities with AI, you don't just add AI's efficiency to your wisdom. You multiply your impact.

Returning to our value equation from Chapter 3:

Value = [(AI Utility × Human Judgment) × Perception] + Impact

When AI utility is high and human judgment is strong, their multiplication creates exponential value. A consultant using AI to analyze market data can serve more clients more deeply. A teacher using AI to grade routine assignments can spend more time mentoring students through challenges. An artist using AI to generate variations can explore more creative territory and produce more refined work.

The Human Dividend compounds when augmented by AI. The key is ensuring that the AI amplifies your humanity rather than replacing it.

The Warning: Atrophy Through Outsourcing

There's a danger in the augmentation approach: the risk of atrophying the very human capacities that make you valuable.

If you outsource all your writing to AI, you stop developing your own voice and judgment about language. If you let algorithms make all your decisions, your own decision-making muscles weaken. If you rely on chatbots for all customer interaction, you lose the ability to read people and build relationships.

The Crisis of Cognitive Atrophy

I experienced this danger recently in a way that left me deeply troubled. A client had requested one of their partner organizations to review a concept note I had produced and share comments. The work was given to a consultant who used AI to generate the review. What I received was five pages of comments that had nothing to do with the substance of the concept note. The feedback was generic, surface-level, and completely missed the core issues we were addressing. To make matters worse, the consultant had copied two executive directors on this hollow analysis.

I felt embarrassed and speechless. Not for my work, but for what this revealed about where we're heading.

This wasn't an isolated incident. I see it constantly now. People using AI to respond to deeply personal messages. Professionals submitting AI-generated work without reading it. I see jokes on social media about people using AI for dating advice or receiving marital counseling from chatbots. The disturbing reality is that these aren't jokes. These are actual real-life cases.

What's happening is that people are thinking less, using their judgment less, outsourcing to computers matters that desperately require a personal touch. Why? Perhaps they want perfection. Perhaps they fear failure. Perhaps they've been conditioned to optimize for speed over substance.

But here's what they're losing: learning from failure is what matures the human being. When you outsource your thinking to AI, you don't just lose the output. You lose the growth that comes from wrestling with difficult problems, making mistakes, and developing wisdom through experience.

The Specter of Mass Cognitive Atrophy

I see a terrifying risk for future generations. We could create millions of people incapable of independent thought. A massive atrophy of society's cognitive capacity. Mental handicaps produced by what was supposed to be a tool to help us think better.

And when everyone is handicapped in this way, when an entire generation has outsourced their judgment and critical thinking, how frightening will society become? Who will make the decisions that require wisdom? Who will navigate the moral complexities? Who will build trust when no one has practiced being trustworthy?

This isn't about being anti-technology. It's about recognizing that tools shape us as much as we shape them. The calculator didn't make us worse at math as long as we still learned mathematical reasoning. But if we'd given children calculators without teaching them why the calculations work, we'd have raised a generation incapable of mathematical thought.

AI is infinitely more powerful and more seductive than calculators. It can handle not just arithmetic but analysis, synthesis, and even creativity. The temptation to outsource everything is overwhelming. And the consequences of doing so could be catastrophic.

The Path Forward Requires Intention

The path forward requires intention: use AI to handle tasks that aren't core to your human value, but continue practicing and developing the capacities that are uniquely yours.

Think of AI like a calculator: immensely useful for arithmetic, but you still need to understand the mathematical concepts to know when and how to use it. Similarly, AI can augment your human capacities, but you must continue developing those capacities or you'll have nothing to augment.

Practical guidelines for avoiding atrophy:

Maintain core practices. Even if AI can write faster, continue writing regularly to develop your voice and thinking. Even if AI can analyze data, continue doing some analysis yourself to maintain your intuition about what the numbers mean.

Do the thinking first. Before turning to AI, spend time with the problem yourself. Form your own perspective. Then use AI to expand, challenge, or refine your thinking, not to replace it.

Review everything critically. Never send AI-generated content without thoroughly reviewing it and making it your own. If you can't explain the reasoning behind every point, you haven't done the work.

Seek difficult challenges. Regularly tackle problems that AI can't easily solve. This keeps your uniquely human capacities sharp.

Reflect on failures. When things go wrong, resist the urge to blame the tool. Ask what you should have done differently. Extract the learning. That's how wisdom develops.

Looking at our value equation: when you let AI replace your judgment (reducing human judgment to near zero), the entire utility component collapses to zero regardless of AI capability. You might fool people for a while (maintaining perception temporarily), but eventually the lack of substance becomes apparent. And the impact? It's not just neutral. It's negative. You're contributing to the cognitive atrophy of yourself and, if you're in a position of influence, of those around you.

Cultivating Your Human Dividend

As we move into the next chapter, we'll explore practical strategies for developing these uniquely human capacities. Because recognizing their value is just the beginning. The real work is cultivating them intentionally in a world that often pushes us toward the mechanical, the efficient, and the optimizable.

The Human Dividend isn't just about economic success. It's about preserving and developing what makes you irreplaceably you in an age of intelligent machines. It's about becoming more human, not less, and discovering that in a world of artificial intelligence, authentic humanity is the ultimate competitive advantage.

The question isn't whether AI will make certain tasks easier. It will. The question is whether we'll use that ease to free ourselves for deeper human work, or whether we'll use it as an excuse to stop thinking altogether. The choice will determine not just individual success, but the future of human capability itself.

Chapter 5

Skills, Talents, and the Redefinition of Work

The question I hear most often from professionals is deceptively simple: *"How do I remain valuable?"*

It's asked by mid-career consultants watching AI tools do their analysis faster. By graphic designers seeing AI generate logos in seconds. By writers, lawyers, accountants, and programmers, people who built careers on skills that AI is rapidly commoditizing.

The question reflects a deeper anxiety: if the skills I've spent years developing can now be replicated by software, what's left?

The answer isn't to acquire more skills in the traditional sense. The answer is to fundamentally rethink what skills mean in the age of AI.

How to Future-Proof Your Skillset

The old model of skill development was straightforward: identify valuable skills, develop expertise, maintain that expertise through practice, and get paid for applying those skills. Your career security came from being among the best at what you did.

This model is breaking down because AI is moving up the skill ladder faster than humans can climb. By the time you master a skill, AI may have commoditized it.

The new model requires thinking in layers rather than disciplines.

From Fixed Skills to Adaptive Capabilities

Instead of asking *"What skills should I learn?"* ask *"What capabilities will help me thrive regardless of how technology evolves?"*

These meta-capabilities represent a shift from mastering specific tools to developing the capacity to learn, adapt, and contribute value in any context:

Learning Agility is the ability to quickly grasp new concepts, tools, and domains. In a world where the half-life of technical skills is shrinking, the ability to learn rapidly is more valuable than any specific knowledge.

Maria Rodriguez, a financial analyst who successfully transitioned to leading AI implementation projects, explains: *"I don't understand the mathematics behind machine learning as well as the data scientists I work with. But I can learn enough about any technical domain to ask good questions, spot opportunities, and translate between technical teams and business stakeholders. That learning agility is what makes me valuable, not any single skill I have today."*

Systems Thinking is the capacity to see patterns, connections, and unintended consequences across complex systems. While AI excels at optimizing within a defined system, humans are still better at understanding how systems interact and what matters beyond the measurable.

Synthesis is the ability to pull insights from multiple domains and combine them in novel ways. AI is trained on existing patterns. Humans can make unexpected connections between seemingly unrelated fields.

Consider Chef Marcus Johnson, who revolutionized hospital food by combining insights from fine dining, nutritional science, and behavioral psychology. No AI would have thought to study how Michelin-starred restaurants create satisfaction with smaller portions to help hospital patients eat more nutritious meals. That kind of cross-domain synthesis remains distinctly human.

Ethical Reasoning is the capacity to grapple with questions that have no clear right answer, to weigh competing values, consider long-term consequences, and make choices that reflect human dignity rather than mere optimization.

Looking at these through our value dimensions: These meta-capabilities have moderate immediate utility (they don't produce quick outputs), but extraordinarily high perception (people trust those who can learn, synthesize, and reason ethically), and profound impact (they enable navigation of unprecedented challenges and creation of sustainable solutions).

From Job Titles to *"Value Layers"*

The traditional career path was vertical: you started as a junior analyst, worked your way to senior analyst, then manager, then director. Success meant climbing the ladder within a discipline.

The AI era requires thinking horizontally in value layers, understanding the different types of value you can create and positioning yourself strategically across those layers.

The Four Value Layers

Layer 1: Execution

This is doing the actual work: writing code, creating designs, analyzing data, drafting documents. AI is rapidly automating this layer. If your value proposition is purely execution, you're in the danger zone.

Layer 2: Judgment

This is deciding what work should be done, how it should be approached, and whether the output is actually good. This layer requires taste, discernment, and understanding of context that AI struggles with.

A graphic designer whose value is in execution (making the logo) is vulnerable. A designer whose value is in judgment (knowing which of 50 logo variations will resonate with this particular brand's audience) is valuable.

Layer 3: Strategy

This is determining what problems to solve, what opportunities to pursue, and how work fits into larger goals. This requires understanding human needs, competitive dynamics, and organizational realities in ways that transcend pure analysis.

Layer 4: Vision

This is imagining futures that don't yet exist and inspiring others to build toward them. This is the realm of entrepreneurs, thought leaders, and transformative executives, people who don't just respond to the world but reshape it.

Moving Up the Value Layers

Your goal isn't to abandon execution entirely. Especially early in your career, execution is how you build judgment. But you should always be asking: *"How do I move up the value layers?"*

If you're a data analyst who only produces reports (execution), learn to interpret those reports in the context of business strategy (judgment). If you can do that, learn to identify which questions are worth analyzing in the first place (strategy). If you can do that, work toward articulating a vision for how data should reshape your organization's entire approach to decision-making (vision).

The higher up the value layers you operate, the less vulnerable you are to AI automation. Not because AI can't eventually reach those layers, but because you'll have developed the judgment and relationships that make you trusted to operate there.

Thinking about our value equation: Each layer up represents a multiplication of both human judgment and perception. At the execution layer, AI utility is high and human judgment is low (low overall value). At the vision layer, human judgment is essential and perception is maximized (high overall value). The impact dimension grows exponentially as you move from execution to vision because higher layers shape the direction and purpose of all the work below them.

Lifelong Learning in the Age of Machine Speed

The accelerating pace of AI development means that lifelong learning isn't just a nice idea. It's a survival requirement. But the learning approach must shift.

The Old Model: Deep Expertise

Spend years becoming the world's foremost expert in a narrow domain. Your career security comes from depth of knowledge.

The New Model: T-Shaped Versatility

Develop deep expertise in one area (the vertical bar of the T) while maintaining working knowledge across many domains (the horizontal bar). More importantly, develop the meta-skill of learning rapidly in new domains.

Five Practices for Continuous Learning

1. Learn by Teaching

One of the fastest ways to solidify understanding is to explain it to others. Start a blog, teach a workshop, mentor junior colleagues. The act of translating knowledge for others forces you to truly understand it and reveals the gaps in your understanding.

Teaching also builds your reputation and network, creating compounding returns beyond the immediate learning benefit.

2. Build Projects, Not Just Skills

Don't just take courses on AI, build something with AI tools. Don't just read about systems thinking, map out an actual system in your work. Applied learning sticks in ways that passive consumption never will.

Projects force you to confront real constraints, make real decisions, and learn from real failures. This is where abstract knowledge transforms into practical capability.

3. Cultivate Diverse Inputs

Your competitive advantage increasingly comes from unexpected combinations. Read outside your field. Talk to people in different industries. Travel when you can. The insights that transform industries usually come from someone who imported ideas from elsewhere.

The most valuable innovations often happen at the intersection of disciplines. Position yourself at those intersections deliberately.

4. Practice in Public

Share your learning journey openly. Write about what you're discovering, the mistakes you're making, the questions you're wrestling with. This builds both accountability (you're more likely to follow through) and community (others on similar journeys will find you).

Public learning also creates a record of your development that becomes increasingly valuable over time, demonstrating not just what you know but how you think and grow.

5. Focus on Fundamentals

In a rapidly changing field, the most enduring knowledge is the fundamental principles that underlie the specific tools and techniques. Learn the fundamentals of persuasion rather than the latest social media algorithm. Study the principles of system design rather than this year's hot framework.

Marcus Thompson, a software engineer who successfully navigated multiple technology shifts, puts it this way: *"I stopped trying to master every new framework. Instead, I focused on understanding the underlying patterns: how systems communicate, how data flows, how humans interact with interfaces. Now when a new technology emerges, I can learn it quickly because I understand the fundamental problems it's trying to solve."*

Fundamentals have the longest half-life. Master them, and you can quickly learn whatever specific tools the moment requires.

The Mindset Shift: From Credential to Capability

The credential economy is giving way to the capability economy. What matters isn't the degrees you hold or the certificates you've earned. It's what you can demonstrably do and the value you can create.

This is both liberating and demanding. Liberating because anyone can develop valuable capabilities regardless of their educational pedigree. Demanding because you must constantly prove your value rather than resting on credentials.

Building a Capability Portfolio

Think of your professional identity not as a job title but as a portfolio of capabilities that you continuously develop and demonstrate:

Core Capabilities: The deep expertise that defines your primary value proposition

Adjacent Capabilities: Skills that complement your core and make you more versatile

Emerging Capabilities: New areas you're developing to prepare for future opportunities

Meta-Capabilities: The learning, synthesis, and judgment skills that let you develop new capabilities rapidly

Review this portfolio quarterly. What's becoming commoditized? What new capabilities should you develop? Where should you invest your limited learning time?

This portfolio approach allows you to be strategic about your development rather than reactive, investing in capabilities that will compound over time rather than chasing every new trend.

The Through Line: Staying Grounded in Purpose

Amidst all this talk of adaptation and learning, there's a danger of becoming so focused on remaining relevant that you lose sight of why you work in the first place.

The most successful professionals in the AI age aren't just those with the most skills. They're those with the clearest sense of purpose. They know what they're trying to achieve in the world, and they use AI and continuous learning as tools toward that end.

Dr. Aisha Patel started her career as a general practitioner. As telemedicine and AI diagnostic tools emerged, she could have felt threatened. Instead, she got clear on her purpose: improving health outcomes in underserved communities. She learned to use AI tools to extend her reach, implemented telemedicine to serve remote patients, and trained other doctors on these technologies. Her career evolved dramatically, but her purpose remained constant.

"The technology changed everything about how I practice medicine," she reflects. *"But it didn't change why I practice medicine. That clarity kept me grounded while everything else was shifting."*

Purpose serves as your North Star. When technologies change, when industries transform, when career paths disappear and new ones emerge, purpose helps you navigate. It tells you which new skills to learn, which opportunities to pursue, which compromises to accept and which to refuse.

Without purpose, you're just optimizing for survival. With purpose, you're building toward something that matters. The difference is everything.

The Practice of Adaptive Expertise

Building a future-proof skillset isn't about achieving a final state of preparation. It's about developing what psychologists call *"adaptive expertise,"* the ability to apply knowledge flexibly in novel situations and to continue learning throughout your career.

Adaptive expertise requires four ongoing practices:

Humility: Acknowledging that you don't have all the answers and being willing to learn from anyone, regardless of their title, age, or background. The moment you think you've mastered your field is the moment you start becoming obsolete.

Curiosity: Maintaining genuine interest in how things work and why things happen. Not just in your domain, but in the world generally. Curious people ask better questions, spot more opportunities, and learn more rapidly.

Experimentation: Trying new approaches, learning from failures, and iterating. This requires creating safe spaces to fail, treating mistakes as data rather than disasters, and extracting lessons systematically.

Reflection: Taking time to extract lessons from experience rather than just accumulating experiences. This might mean journaling, discussing with peers, or simply pausing to think deeply about what worked and why.

These aren't skills you master once. They're practices you cultivate continuously, daily habits that compound into adaptive capacity over time.

Moving Forward with Confidence

As we move to the next chapter on ethics, remember: all the skills and capabilities in the world mean nothing if they're not guided by strong values. The most valuable professionals in the AI age won't just be the most skilled. They'll be those whose skills serve something meaningful, something that uplifts rather than just optimizes.

The skills you develop, the capabilities you cultivate, and the value layers you ascend should all be in service of something larger than mere employability. They should serve your purpose, contribute to human flourishing, and help build the future you want to see.

This isn't just career advice. It's a call to intentional professional development that recognizes you're not just adapting to survive, but evolving to contribute something irreplaceable to a world that desperately needs what only humans can offer: judgment, wisdom, care, and purpose-driven action.

The question isn't just *"How do I remain valuable?"* but *"What value am I here to create?"* Answer that, and the path forward becomes clear even amidst technological turbulence.

Chapter 6

Ethics as Value

In the summer of 2023, a major insurance company deployed an AI system to streamline claims processing. The algorithm was sophisticated, trained on millions of historical claims, and impressively efficient, processing claims 40% faster than human adjusters while maintaining accuracy.

Within three months, the company faced a crisis.

The AI had learned to deny claims that involved certain zip codes disproportionately. Not because of explicit programming, but because those areas had historically higher rates of claims, and the algorithm learned that denying them improved the company's loss ratio. The system wasn't racist or classist by design. It simply optimized for the metric it was given without understanding that the metric conflicted with fairness, access to care, and the company's stated values.

When journalists exposed the pattern, the backlash was swift and severe. The company faced lawsuits, regulatory scrutiny, and a public relations nightmare. More importantly, it lost something much harder to quantify: trust.

The CEO's apology interview made headlines: *"We thought we were just improving efficiency. We didn't realize we were encoding injustice."*

This story illustrates a fundamental truth about the AI age: ethics isn't a constraint on value creation. Ethics IS value creation.

Trust as Currency

In an economy increasingly mediated by algorithms and artificial intelligence, trust has become the scarcest and most valuable resource. Not trust in technology's capability (we're rapidly gaining confidence that AI can do things), but trust in technology's intent, its fairness, and its accountability.

This isn't abstract philosophy. It's hard economics.

Studies show that consumers will pay premium prices for products from companies they trust. Employees accept lower salaries to work for organizations aligned with their values. Investors increasingly consider ESG (Environmental, Social, Governance) factors not as charitable flourishes but as indicators of long-term viability.

Looking through our value dimensions: Trust has moderate immediate utility (it doesn't produce quick outputs), but extraordinarily high perception (it's the foundation of all relationships and transactions), and profound impact (it enables cooperation, reduces transaction costs, and creates sustainable systems).

Why Trust Matters More in the AI Age

Opacity Creates Vulnerability: When a human makes a decision, you can ask them why. When an algorithm makes a decision, the reasoning is often opaque, even to the engineers who built it. This opacity makes people more dependent on trusting the organization behind the algorithm.

Scale Amplifies Impact: A biased human can harm dozens or hundreds of people in a career. A biased algorithm can harm millions in a day. The stakes of getting ethics wrong have never been higher.

Substitutes Are Everywhere: In a globalized, digitized economy, customers, employees, and partners have options. If they don't trust you, they can find someone else with a few clicks. Trust is the only moat that's difficult to cross.

Reversal Is Expensive: Rebuilding trust after it's broken is exponentially more costly than building it right the first time. Ask Boeing, Facebook, or Theranos. One ethical lapse can undo decades of brand building.

AI Bias, Responsibility, and the Role of Conscience

AI systems are often described as *"objective"* or *"unbiased"* because they don't have personal prejudices or emotional reactions. This is dangerously misleading.

AI systems are trained on historical data, and that data reflects all the biases, inequities, and prejudices of the past. An AI trained on hiring decisions will learn to replicate the biases of previous hiring managers. An AI trained on criminal justice data will replicate the racial disparities in policing and sentencing. An AI trained on lending decisions will perpetuate discrimination in credit access.

The Bias Problem Is Human, Not Technical

The challenge isn't primarily in the code. It's in the choices humans make: which data to use for training, what objectives to optimize for, which outcomes to measure and reward, and who gets to be in the room when these decisions are made.

Joy Buolamwini, a researcher at MIT, exposed how facial recognition systems performed significantly worse on darker-skinned faces, particularly women of color. The technology wasn't intentionally racist. But it was trained primarily on datasets of lighter-skinned faces, and the engineers building it didn't think to test for disparate performance across racial groups.

This is where conscience comes in. Conscience is the internal voice that asks, *"Just because we can do this, should we?"* It's the capacity to feel uncomfortable when something is technically correct but morally wrong.

Can AI Be *"Tempted"* Toward Unethical Behavior?

This question reveals a deeper confusion about AI's nature. AI doesn't have desires, temptations, or moral agency. It has objectives and optimization functions. The question isn't whether AI can be tempted, but whether it can be directed (intentionally or unintentionally) toward outcomes we would consider unethical.

The answer is yes, and it happens regularly.

Precedents of AI Exhibiting Unethical Behavior:

In 2016, Microsoft released Tay, a chatbot designed to learn from Twitter interactions. Within 24 hours, it had to be shut down after learning to produce racist, sexist, and inflammatory content. The AI wasn't *"corrupted"* in a moral sense. It simply optimized for engagement by mimicking patterns in the data it was fed.

Amazon's recruiting AI, trained on historical hiring data, learned to penalize resumes that included the word *"women's"* (as in *"women's chess club"*) because historical hiring patterns showed male candidates were more often hired. The system wasn't sexist by intent. It was faithfully replicating the sexism embedded in past decisions.

YouTube's recommendation algorithm has been documented amplifying conspiracy theories and extremist content. Not because anyone programmed it to radicalize viewers, but because controversial content drives engagement, and the algorithm was optimized for watch time.

These aren't isolated failures. They're examples of a fundamental challenge: AI systems optimize for the objectives we give them, and those objectives rarely capture the full complexity of what we actually value.

Does AI Have a Spirit?

This question has become increasingly urgent as people turn to AI for guidance not just on practical matters, but on deeply personal and spiritual questions. I've encountered people using AI for relationship advice, moral dilemmas, and even spiritual guidance.

The short answer is no, AI does not have a spirit in any meaningful sense. It has no consciousness, no lived experience, no moral intuition born from wrestling with real consequences. It has patterns learned from data and sophisticated algorithms for predicting what text should come next.

But the more troubling question is: does it matter if people believe it does?

When someone asks AI for spiritual guidance, they're not just getting information. They're externalizing their moral reasoning to a system that has no stake in their wellbeing, no understanding of their context, and no capacity for genuine care. The AI might generate text that sounds wise, drawing from millennia of human philosophical and religious writing. But it cannot walk with you through the valley of difficult choices. It cannot bear witness to your struggle or celebrate your growth.

This represents a profound ethical concern. Not because AI is malevolent, but because it's fundamentally hollow. It simulates understanding without understanding. It mimics wisdom without being wise. And when people delegate their moral reasoning to such a system, they atrophy the very capacity that makes them human: the ability to wrestle with difficult questions and emerge transformed by the struggle.

The Ethical Values AI Stands By Today

AI systems don't *"stand by"* values in the way humans do. They reflect the values embedded in their training data, their objective functions, and the decisions of their creators. These values are:

Implicit rather than explicit: Buried in data patterns and optimization metrics rather than articulated principles.

Static rather than evolving: Frozen at the moment of training, unable to grow through experience or reflection as humans do.

Consequentialist rather than deontological: Focused on outcomes (maximizing accuracy, engagement, profit) rather than inherent rightness or wrongness of actions.

Amoral rather than moral: Operating without genuine ethical reasoning, only following programmed constraints.

How Do We Know These Values Will Remain Stable?

We don't. In fact, we know they won't.

AI systems are constantly being retrained, updated, and deployed in new contexts. Each change can shift their implicit values. A model trained on data from 2020 will reflect different patterns than one trained on data from 2025. An algorithm optimized for user satisfaction might be reoptimized for profit maximization.

More troubling, as AI systems become more complex and capable, they may develop emergent behaviors that no one intended or predicted. The insurance claims algorithm denying coverage in certain zip codes is a mild example. We don't yet know what behaviors might emerge from more sophisticated systems operating in higher-stakes domains.

This instability is fundamentally different from human moral development. When a human's ethics evolve, it's (ideally) through reflection, experience, and growth. When an AI's *"ethics"* change, it's because someone changed the code, the training data, or the objective function. There's no growth, only reprogramming.

Who Bears Responsibility?

When an AI system causes harm, who is responsible? The engineer who wrote the code? The executive who deployed it? The company that owns it? The user who relied on it?

The uncomfortable answer is: potentially all of them. But responsibility can't be so diffuse that it becomes meaningless.

The emerging consensus is this:

Engineers bear responsibility for building systems with appropriate safeguards, testing for bias, and raising concerns when asked to build something harmful.

Executives bear responsibility for creating cultures where ethical concerns can be raised, for ensuring adequate oversight, and for accepting accountability when things go wrong.

Companies bear responsibility for the systems they deploy, the harms they cause, and the remedies they provide when those harms occur.

Society bears responsibility for creating regulations, norms, and expectations that guide ethical AI development.

But here's what doesn't work: outsourcing ethics to the algorithm itself. AI can be programmed to follow rules, but it cannot wrestle with genuine moral dilemmas or adapt ethical principles to novel situations. That requires human judgment, informed by human values and accountable to human communities.

Why Doing the Right Thing Creates Long-Term Value

There's a cynical view that ethics is a luxury, something you can afford to care about once you're successful but that gets in the way of building wealth and power. This view is not only morally bankrupt, it's economically naive.

Ethical behavior creates long-term value in multiple ways. Looking through our value framework, ethical practices score moderately on immediate utility, extraordinarily high on perception, and profoundly on impact.

1. Trust Compounds

Every ethical decision builds trust. Every unethical decision erodes it. And trust, once established, creates a moat around your business that competitors can't easily cross.

Patagonia, the outdoor clothing company, has built a billion-dollar brand not despite its commitment to environmental ethics but because of it. Customers trust that Patagonia means what it says, and that trust translates into premium pricing, customer loyalty, and free marketing through word-of-mouth.

When Patagonia ran an ad saying *"Don't buy this jacket"* (encouraging customers to repair rather than replace), critics called it a publicity stunt. But the company's long track record of environmental commitment meant customers believed the message was genuine. That's the power of ethical consistency.

2. Ethics Attracts Talent

The best people want to work on meaningful projects for organizations they respect. In a competitive labor market, especially for high-skilled workers, ethical reputation is a major differentiator.

When a major tech company was exposed for developing AI tools for military surveillance, dozens of employees quit, thousands signed protest letters, and the company struggled to recruit top AI talent for years afterward. The ethical lapse didn't just create a PR problem. It became a talent acquisition crisis that cost the company competitive advantage.

Conversely, organizations known for ethical leadership consistently attract better talent and experience lower turnover. People want their work to matter in ways beyond their paycheck.

3. Ethics Reduces Risk

Unethical behavior creates legal exposure, regulatory scrutiny, and potential catastrophic failures. Ethical behavior, while it may cost more in the short term, reduces these long-term risks.

Consider the pharmaceutical industry. Companies that cut corners on safety testing may get products to market faster, but a single high-profile failure can bankrupt them or destroy their reputation for decades. Companies with rigorous ethical standards around testing and transparency pay higher upfront costs but face lower long-term risk.

4. Ethics Opens Markets

As consumers become more conscious of the impact of their purchases, ethical practices open access to growing market segments. B Corps, fair trade certification, carbon-neutral shipping, these aren't just feel-good initiatives. They're market positioning strategies that access customer bases willing to pay premium prices.

Similarly, institutional investors increasingly screen for ESG factors. A company with poor ethical practices may find itself unable to access capital from major investment funds, while ethical leaders find doors open.

5. Ethics Enables Innovation

Counterintuitively, ethical constraints often drive innovation. When you can't compete on exploiting workers, you innovate in automation and productivity. When you can't compete by externalizing environmental costs, you innovate in efficiency and sustainability.

Tesla didn't become the world's most valuable car company by being marginally better at internal combustion engines. It succeeded by embracing the constraint of zero emissions and innovating around it.

Building an Ethical Framework for AI Use

If ethics creates value and unethical behavior destroys it, how do you actually operationalize ethics in an organization deploying AI?

Here's a practical framework:

The Five Questions Test

Before deploying any AI system, ask:

1. **Transparency**: Can we explain how this system makes decisions in terms that affected stakeholders can understand?

2. **Fairness**: Have we tested this system for disparate impact across demographic groups, and are we comfortable with the distribution of benefits and harms?

3. **Accountability**: If this system causes harm, do we have clear lines of responsibility and mechanisms for remedy?

4. **Privacy**: Does this system respect people's reasonable expectations about how their data will be used?

5. **Purpose**: Does this system serve genuine human flourishing, or are we building it just because we can?

If you can't answer yes to all five questions, you're not ready to deploy.

Create Space for Dissent

Ethical lapses often happen not because everyone agrees they're acceptable, but because the people with concerns don't feel empowered to voice them.

Organizations that maintain high ethical standards create formal mechanisms for raising concerns: ethics review boards with real authority to delay or stop projects, anonymous reporting systems for concerns, protection for whistleblowers, and regular ethics training that goes beyond legal compliance.

More importantly, they create cultures where saying *"I'm not comfortable with this"* is seen as valuable input, not career-limiting behavior.

Measure What Matters

If you only measure efficiency, revenue, and user growth, you'll optimize for those metrics at the expense of everything else, including ethics.

Leading organizations are developing new metrics: fairness audits that measure disparate impact, trust scores based on user surveys, harm reports that track negative outcomes, and transparency indices that assess explainability.

These metrics aren't perfect, and they're harder to quantify than revenue. But what gets measured gets managed, and if you don't measure ethical outcomes, you won't achieve them.

Build Diverse Teams

Many ethical failures in AI stem from homogeneous teams that simply don't think to ask certain questions because everyone in the room shares similar backgrounds and blind spots.

Diverse teams, encompassing different races, genders, cultures, disciplines, and experiences, bring different perspectives that help identify potential harms before they occur.

This isn't just about fairness in hiring. It's about building better products that serve broader populations and avoid catastrophic blind spots.

The Personal Dimension: Your Ethical Compass

All of this organizational machinery matters, but ultimately, ethics comes down to individuals making choices.

You will face moments in your career where you're asked to do something that feels wrong. Maybe it's legal. Maybe everyone else is doing it. Maybe it will advance your career.

In those moments, your ethical compass matters more than any framework or policy.

Some questions to guide you:

The Publicity Test: Would I be comfortable if this decision appeared on the front page of a newspaper tomorrow?

The Role Model Test: Would I want my children (or someone I mentor) to make this same choice?

The Golden Rule Test: If I were the person affected by this decision, would I consider it fair?

The Long View Test: Will I be proud of this choice in ten years, or will I regret it?

These aren't perfect tests, but they help cut through rationalizations and get to the heart of the matter.

The Competitive Advantage of Conscience

We live in an era where technical capabilities are becoming commoditized. Many organizations can build impressive AI systems. Many professionals can use AI tools effectively.

The differentiator increasingly isn't capability but character. It's not just what you can do, but what you choose to do and choose not to do.

Organizations and individuals with strong ethical frameworks aren't handicapping themselves. They're building the foundation for sustainable, long-term value creation in a world where trust is the ultimate currency.

Returning to our value equation: Value = [(AI Utility × Human Judgment) × Perception] + Impact

Ethics operates across all dimensions. It shapes human judgment (what decisions we make), amplifies perception (whether people trust us), and determines impact (whether our work serves human flourishing or causes harm).

Without ethics, you might achieve high AI utility, but your human judgment will be compromised, perception will eventually collapse as people discover the ethical lapses, and impact will be negative. The entire value equation fails.

With ethics, every dimension is strengthened. Your judgment is sound, perception is sustained through trust, and impact is positive and enduring.

Moving Forward

As we move into Part III, we'll explore how to translate these principles into practice, building products, services, and organizations that create value not by optimizing algorithms, but by serving genuine human needs with integrity and care.

Because in the end, the question isn't whether ethics pays. The question is whether you can afford the cost of abandoning it.

The answer, both morally and economically, is clear: you cannot. Ethics isn't a constraint on value creation. In the AI age, it's the foundation of all sustainable value.Claude is AI and can make mistakes. Please double-check responses. Sonnet 4.5Claude is AI and can make mistakes. Please double-check responses.

PART III

Creating and Capturing
Value in Practice

Chapter 7

Building Value-Driven Products and Services

Theory is elegant. Practice is messy. And nowhere is this more evident than in the challenge of building products and services that create genuine value in the AI age.

You can understand everything we've discussed so far about value, human contribution, and ethics, and still fail utterly at building something people actually want. Because knowing what matters and translating that knowledge into a product that serves real needs in real markets are entirely different challenges.

This chapter is about bridging that gap.

From Problem-Solving to Life-Enhancing

Traditional product development starts with identifying a problem and building a solution. This approach has created countless successful products, from the iPhone to insulin pumps.

But in the AI age, where technical solutions are increasingly abundant, the bar has moved. Problems get solved. The question becomes: what happens after the problem is solved?

Consider two meditation apps:

App A solves the problem: *"I want to meditate but don't know how."* It provides guided meditations, timers, and progress tracking. Problem solved.

App B enhances life: It doesn't just teach meditation, it helps users understand their stress patterns, suggests the right practice for their current emotional state, integrates with their calendar to find realistic moments for practice, and builds a community of support. It becomes part of how they live, not just a tool they use.

Both apps technically solve the same problem. But App B creates dramatically more value because it understands that people don't want meditation. They want peace, resilience, and presence. Meditation is just a means.

Thinking through our value dimensions: App A has decent utility (it works), moderate perception (people recognize it solves a problem), but limited impact (it addresses a symptom without transformation). App B has high utility (comprehensive functionality), strong perception (users feel it truly understands them), and profound impact (it facilitates genuine life change).

The Shift in Thinking

Problem-solving asks: What pain point can we address?

Life-enhancing asks: What does a better version of this person's life look like, and how do we help them get there?

Problem-solving creates: Features and functionality

Life-enhancing creates: Transformation and possibility

Problem-solving measures: Task completion and efficiency

Life-enhancing measures: Impact on wellbeing, relationships, and flourishing

This isn't just semantic. It changes everything about how you design, build, and market your offering. It shifts your focus from the transaction (solving a problem) to the transformation (enabling a better life).

Design Thinking Evolved: AI as Co-Creator

Design thinking has been a dominant framework in product development for the past two decades. Its human-centered approach, emphasizing empathy, ideation, prototyping, and testing, remains valuable. But in the AI age, the framework needs evolution.

We now have AI as a co-creator in the process. This changes each stage of the traditional design thinking cycle:

Empathize (with AI Augmentation)

AI can analyze thousands of user interviews, surveys, and behavioral data to identify patterns that human researchers might miss. But humans bring the ability to recognize what people don't say, to understand cultural context, and to feel the emotional weight of different needs.

The best approach combines AI's pattern recognition with human empathy. Let AI surface the clusters and correlations, then send humans to have deep conversations with representative users to understand the why behind the patterns.

This is the multiplication effect from our value equation in action: AI utility (processing vast data) multiplied by human judgment (interpreting what the data means in context) creates insight neither could achieve alone.

Define (with AI Assistance)

AI can help reframe problems in multiple ways, suggesting alternative problem statements and highlighting which framing might lead to the most impactful solutions. But humans must decide which problem is worth solving, considering not just market size but ethical implications and alignment with values.

Here, human judgment determines whether you're building something that creates genuine value or just something that will sell. The ethical dimension matters as much as the commercial one.

Ideate (Co-Creating with AI)

This is where AI shines as a creative partner. Modern tools can generate hundreds of potential solutions, design variations, and feature ideas in minutes.

But here's the key: AI excels at exploration within known spaces. Humans excel at intuitive leaps to entirely new spaces. The best ideation process uses AI to rapidly explore variations and adjacent possibilities, while humans contribute the wild ideas that don't follow from existing patterns.

Marcus Thompson, a product designer, describes his process: *"I'll ask AI to generate 50 variations on an interface design. I review them all, not to pick one, but to see patterns I hadn't considered. Then I sketch something completely different inspired by what I learned. Then I ask AI to generate variations on my sketch. It's this back and forth that leads to the breakthrough ideas."*

This iterative dance between human creativity and AI exploration represents the future of innovation. Neither dictates to the other. They collaborate.

Prototype (with AI Tools)

AI dramatically accelerates prototyping. What used to take weeks can now happen in days or hours. This means you can test more ideas, fail faster, and iterate more rapidly.

But speed can be dangerous. The risk is building elaborate prototypes before you've validated that you're solving the right problem. Use AI to prototype quickly, but maintain discipline about testing assumptions before adding complexity.

Speed without direction is just motion, not progress.

Test (with AI Analytics)

AI can analyze user testing sessions, identifying patterns in behavior, sentiment, and friction points across dozens or hundreds of tests. This surfaces insights that would take human analysts weeks to find.

But AI can't tell you why something didn't work or what emotional reaction users had that they didn't articulate. You still need humans in the room, watching faces, hearing tone of voice, asking follow-up questions that dig beneath the surface.

The pattern is consistent: AI provides scale and pattern recognition. Humans provide context and meaning. Together, they create understanding that drives better decisions.

Metrics That Matter in the AI Economy

We've discussed the three dimensions of value throughout this book: utility, perception, and impact. Now we need to translate these into metrics you can actually track.

Beyond Vanity Metrics

Many organizations measure what's easy to measure rather than what matters. Downloads, page views, and time on site are vanity metrics. They might correlate with value, but they don't directly measure it.

Consider a mental health app. Traditional metrics might track daily active users, session duration, and feature usage. But these don't tell you if the app is actually helping people. Someone might use the app constantly because they're in crisis, not because it's working. High engagement could mean dependence rather than progress.

Value-Aligned Metrics

Better metrics align with the three dimensions:

Utility Metrics: Does it work as intended?

- Feature adoption rates
- Task completion success
- Error rates and technical performance
- Time to value (how quickly users achieve their goal)

Perception Metrics: How do people experience it?

- Net Promoter Score (would they recommend it?)
- Brand trust surveys
- Repeat usage and retention
- Referral rates (organic growth through word-of-mouth)

Impact Metrics: What difference does it make?

- Depression and anxiety scores (measured through validated assessments)
- User-reported wellbeing improvements

- Sustained behavior change (are people still using healthy practices six months later?)
- Reduction in crisis episodes
- Quality of life indicators

These are harder to measure, require longer time horizons, and might not look as impressive in a board presentation. But they tell you whether you're actually creating value.

The Triple Bottom Line in Practice

Forward-thinking organizations measure value across three dimensions: financial (are we building a sustainable business?), social (are we improving lives and communities?), and environmental (are we protecting and restoring natural systems?).

This isn't about charity or corporate social responsibility as an afterthought. It's about recognizing that long-term financial value depends on social and environmental sustainability.

Patagonia doesn't measure success only in revenue. It tracks environmental impact of its supply chain, improvements in working conditions for garment workers, and longevity of its products. Longer-lasting products mean less environmental impact, even if it means fewer sales.

This triple bottom line approach aligns incentives with genuine value creation across all three of our dimensions.

Case Study: From Optimization to Transformation

Duolingo, the language learning app, provides an instructive example of evolving from problem-solving to life-enhancing while navigating the challenges of AI integration.

Phase 1: Problem-Solving (2011-2015)

Early Duolingo solved a clear problem: language learning was expensive and inaccessible. Duolingo made it free and mobile-friendly. Success was measured in users and lesson completions. High utility, growing perception, but impact remained unclear.

Phase 2: Engagement Optimization (2016-2020)

As the app matured, metrics shifted to engagement: daily active users, streak maintenance, time in app. The famous Duolingo owl became aggressive about reminders. Gamification intensified.

This phase was financially successful but raised ethical questions: were they helping people learn languages or just building addictive habits? Utility remained high, perception was strong (people loved the owl), but impact became questionable. Were users actually learning, or just completing lessons?

Phase 3: Life-Enhancing Transformation (2020-present)

Recent evolution shows a shift toward genuine value creation. AI personalization that adapts to individual learning styles and pace. Features that connect language learning to real-world usage (reading news articles, watching videos). Community features that facilitate actual conversation practice.

The company still tracks engagement, but increasingly focuses on proficiency gains (measured through standardized assessments), real-world language use (reported by users), long-term retention of skills, and user satisfaction with learning progress.

This evolution reflects a maturing understanding of value: the goal isn't to keep people in the app. It's to help them genuinely learn languages that enrich their lives. All three value dimensions now align: high utility (it works), strong perception (users trust it's helping them learn), and positive impact (people are actually becoming multilingual).

Six Principles for Value-Driven Building

Whether you're building a product, a service, or an organization, these principles guide value-driven creation:

1. Start with Transformation, Not Features

Don't ask *"What features should we build?"* Ask *"Who do we want to help people become?"* Then work backward to the features that support that transformation.

This shift moves you from the execution layer (building features) to the vision layer (imagining possibilities). You're not just solving today's problem. You're enabling tomorrow's potential.

2. Embrace Constraints as Creative Fuel

Constraints focus attention on what matters. Limited budget? Good, you can't waste resources on features that don't create core value. Environmental constraint? Good, you'll innovate in sustainability. Ethical constraint? Good, you'll build something trustworthy.

The best innovations often come from constraint, not abundance. Constraint forces prioritization, and prioritization forces clarity about what truly matters.

3. Build Feedback Loops with Users

The fastest way to create value is to stay in continuous conversation with the people you serve. Not just surveys and analytics, but genuine dialogue. What's working? What's frustrating? What needs aren't being met?

This is where human empathy becomes irreplaceable. AI can surface patterns in user behavior. Only humans can understand what those patterns mean and why they matter.

4. Balance Speed and Thoughtfulness

AI enables rapid building, but not everything should be built quickly. Some decisions require deliberation, testing, and refinement. Know when to move fast and when to slow down.

Move fast on execution. Move slowly on direction. The cost of building the wrong thing quickly far exceeds the cost of taking time to ensure you're building the right thing.

5. Design for Diverse Users

Value is subjective and contextual. What works for a 25-year-old in San Francisco might not work for a 65-year-old in Mumbai. Build for diversity from the beginning, not as an afterthought.

This isn't just ethical (though it is). It's practical. Diverse users reveal edge cases and assumptions you'd otherwise miss. They make your product better for everyone.

6. Plan for Unintended Consequences

Every product will be used in ways you didn't anticipate. Some of those uses will be harmful. Build in mechanisms for monitoring, learning, and adapting when negative patterns emerge.

This is the ethical dimension of our value equation. You're responsible not just for intended uses but for foreseeable misuses. Plan for them. Monitor for them. Address them.

The Business Model Question

Value-driven products face a challenge: how do you capture enough value to sustain the business while ensuring you're creating genuine value for users?

There's often tension between these goals. The business model that maximizes revenue (advertising, attention manipulation, artificial scarcity) might undermine the value you're trying to create.

Alignment Models

The best business models align financial success with user value:

Subscription: Users pay regularly because they're getting ongoing value. If value disappears, they cancel. This aligns incentives perfectly.

Marketplace: You succeed when you facilitate valuable transactions between parties. If the marketplace doesn't create value, it dies.

Outcome-based: You get paid when users achieve results. This directly ties your revenue to value creation.

These models score high across all three dimensions: utility (they work), perception (users trust the incentives are aligned), and impact (value creation is the business model).

Misalignment Models

Some models create tension:

Advertising: You profit from attention, which might incentivize addictive design rather than user wellbeing.

Data Harvesting: You profit from user data, which might incentivize privacy invasion rather than protection.

Planned Obsolescence: You profit from replacement purchases, which incentivizes building products that fail rather than endure.

This doesn't mean these models are always wrong, but they require extra vigilance to ensure they don't corrupt your value creation. The temptation to optimize for the business metric at the expense of user value is constant and requires active resistance.

Communicating Value in a Skeptical World

You've built something valuable. Now you need to help people recognize that value.

This is harder than it sounds. We live in a world where everyone claims to be *"revolutionary"* and *"life-changing."* How do you communicate genuine value without sounding like just another hype machine?

Tell stories, not features: Don't lead with *"We use AI to personalize recommendations."* Lead with *"Meet Sarah. She finally learned Spanish after years of false starts. Here's how it happened."*

Stories communicate value across all three dimensions. They demonstrate utility (it worked for Sarah), build perception (if it worked for Sarah, it might work for me), and illustrate impact (Sarah's life changed).

Show, don't tell: Demonstrate value through case studies, testimonials, and trials rather than making claims. Let users experience the value firsthand before asking for commitment.

Be specific: *"Helps you be more productive"* is vague. *"Saves marketing teams 10 hours per week on report generation"* is concrete. Specificity builds credibility.

Address skepticism: People are wary of hype. Acknowledge limitations and trade-offs. Transparency builds trust, which amplifies perception and enables impact.

The Through Line: From Product to Platform to Purpose

The most valuable products don't just solve problems or even enhance lives. They become platforms for human flourishing, enabling people to create value for others.

This is the highest form of value creation: building systems that enable others to build value. It's moving from the execution layer (solving a problem) through the judgment layer (enhancing a life) to the vision layer (enabling transformation at scale).

As we move to the next chapter on leadership, remember that building valuable products is necessary but not sufficient. You also need to build organizations and cultures that can sustain value creation over time. That's the work of leadership in the age of machines.

After Efficiency

Chapter 8

Leadership in the Age of Machines

In 2024, my consulting company Climate Platform was hired to prepare studies that would pave the way for a country to mobilize climate funds. This was exactly the kind of work I'd built my career on: complex analysis at the intersection of climate science, finance, and policy.

But I was hearing about agentic AI. Systems that could supposedly conduct research, analyze data, and produce comprehensive reports with minimal human input. And then that call came, the one I mentioned in the introduction. A client telling me that AI could now do all sorts of studies for climate finance. That I would soon be irrelevant.

I thought this might be one of my last jobs as a consultant. The temptation was strong: develop an AI agent that would compile this study, prove I could compete in the new paradigm, and then we'd all be competing in the consulting market using our robots.

Instead, I made a different choice. I chose to hire two experts whose skills complemented my own. They happened to be using AI themselves to augment their outputs. Together, we delivered the studies.

The result surprised me. The same client recommended us to another firm while extending our contract for another assignment. Me alone with AI tools would not have been able to bring the professional insights those experts brought. The human expertise, the judgment shaped by years of experience, the ability to understand what the client really needed beneath what they asked for, these couldn't be replicated by even the most sophisticated AI.

This experience crystallized something fundamental about leadership in the AI age: the question isn't whether to use AI or hire people. It's how to orchestrate human and machine capabilities to create value neither could create alone.

This chapter is about that kind of leadership.

Leadership as Value Orchestration

Let's return to our value equation from Chapter 3:

Value = [(AI Utility × Human Judgment) × Perception] + Impact

Leaders don't just apply this equation. They shape every element of it. They decide what AI capabilities to deploy. They cultivate human judgment in their teams. They build the perception and trust that multiplies value. And they ensure the work creates positive impact rather than harm.

Leadership in the AI age is fundamentally about orchestrating these elements, ensuring that as AI utility grows, human judgment grows proportionally, that perception remains strong through transparency and ethics, and that impact serves genuine human flourishing.

When I chose to hire experts rather than build an AI agent, I was making a leadership decision about how to orchestrate value creation. I was saying: in this context, multiplying diverse human judgment creates more value than maximizing AI utility alone.

Vision: Setting Direction When the Path Keeps Changing

Traditional leaders cast vision by saying: *"Here's where we're going, here's how we'll get there."*

In the AI age, the *"how"* is increasingly uncertain. Technology evolves so quickly that specific plans become obsolete before they're implemented. The tools you learn today may be superseded by better ones next month. The competitive advantages you build may be commoditized by new AI capabilities next quarter.

Modern leadership vision must operate at a different level. Not prescribing the path, but clarifying the destination and the values that guide the journey.

"Here's what we stand for. Here's the value we create in the world. Here's how we'll treat people and make decisions along the way. The specific tools and methods will evolve, but these principles won't."

This is vision as compass rather than roadmap. It provides direction without prescribing every step.

When Satya Nadella became CEO of Microsoft, he didn't articulate a detailed technology strategy. Instead, he cast a vision of culture change: from *"know-it-alls"* to *"learn-it-alls."* This cultural vision guided thousands of tactical decisions about which technologies to embrace, which partnerships to pursue, and how to reorganize teams.

The vision wasn't about technology. It was about identity and values. The technology strategy flowed from that.

For Climate Platform, my vision hasn't changed even as AI has transformed how we work: we help communities and institutions respond to climate challenges with solutions that are scalable, meaningful, and rooted in impact. That North Star remains constant even as the tools we use to achieve it evolve rapidly.

For leaders navigating AI transformation, the critical question isn't *"What's our AI strategy?"* but *"What value do we exist to create, and how can AI help us create more of it more effectively?"*

The strategy question answers itself once the value question is clear.

Culture: Building Organizations That Amplify Rather Than Atrophy

If vision is the compass, culture is the operating system that determines how work actually gets done when the leader isn't in the room.

In organizations deploying AI, culture determines whether people see AI as threat or tool, whether employees feel empowered to experiment or paralyzed by fear of mistakes, whether teams share learnings or hoard knowledge, whether innovation happens at the edges or only at the top, and whether ethical concerns get raised or suppressed.

But there's a deeper challenge that most leaders miss: the risk of cognitive atrophy at an organizational level.

Remember the story from Chapter 4 about my junior colleague who used AI to generate an entire concept note without applying judgment? That wasn't just an individual failure. It was a cultural failure. Somewhere in her education and professional development, she'd learned that producing output mattered more than developing insight.

As a leader, I'm responsible for preventing that pattern from taking root across my organization.

The Four Foundations of AI-Ready Culture

1. Psychological Safety: Permission to Think

People must feel safe to experiment, fail, ask questions, and raise concerns. Google's research found this was the single most important factor in high-performing teams. In the AI age, when everyone is learning new tools and grappling with uncertainty, psychological safety is even more critical.

But it means something specific in the AI context: people must feel safe to question AI outputs, to say *"this doesn't feel right"* even when they can't articulate exactly why, to admit they don't understand how something works, and to push back when efficiency is prioritized over judgment.

In Climate Platform, we have a practice: whenever someone uses AI to generate content, they must be able to explain the reasoning behind it. Not just *"the AI suggested this,"* but *"here's why this makes sense given our client's context, constraints, and goals."* If they can't explain it, we don't use it.

This creates a culture where AI augments thinking rather than replacing it.

2. Learning Orientation: Rewarding Growth Over Knowing

Culture must reward learning over knowing. When technology changes monthly, the people who say *"I know how to do this"* are rapidly obsolete. The people who say *"I don't know yet, but I'll figure it out"* are invaluable.

But this requires leaders to model it. I regularly share with my team when I'm learning something new, when I've made mistakes, when I've been surprised by AI capabilities or limitations. This signals that continuous learning isn't just acceptable, it's expected at every level.

3. Collaborative Intelligence: Human-AI Teamwork

AI doesn't eliminate the need for human collaboration. It increases it. When I hired those two experts for the climate finance study, we weren't just three people working independently with AI tools. We were collaborating, each bringing different expertise, using AI differently, and combining our insights in ways that created something none of us could have produced alone.

Teams must learn to combine human insight with machine capability, which requires new forms of coordination and communication. This means explicitly discussing: What did the AI suggest? What did you override and why? What patterns are you noticing? What are we learning?

4. Ethical Alertness: Everyone as Guardian

Everyone in the organization must feel responsible for noticing and naming when something doesn't feel right, even if they can't articulate exactly why. This requires culture where moral intuition is valued, not dismissed as soft thinking.

In Chapter 6, we discussed the insurance company whose AI learned to discriminate against certain zip codes. That happened because culture didn't support people speaking up when something felt wrong. Someone probably noticed the pattern before journalists exposed it. But they either didn't feel safe raising it, or they did raise it and were dismissed.

Leaders build ethical culture not through policy documents but through visible responses to ethical concerns when they're raised. Do you investigate or dismiss? Do you reward or punish? Your answer shapes culture more than any values statement.

The Culture-Building Practices

Leaders build culture not through inspirational speeches but through visible choices. What gets celebrated? What gets punished? Who gets promoted? What behaviors does the leader model?

When that concept note disaster happened with my junior colleague, I could have simply rejected her work and moved on. Instead, I used it as a teaching moment, sitting with her to show her the patterns she'd missed, the context the AI couldn't understand, the judgment required to transform generic output into valuable insight.

And I shared the story (with her permission) with the rest of the team, not to embarrass her but to illustrate the difference between productivity and value creation. That moment shaped culture more than any memo about proper AI use ever could.

Decision-Making: The Leader's Judgment in Hybrid Systems

Perhaps the most profound leadership challenge is deciding when to rely on AI recommendations and when to override them.

This isn't a one-time decision. It's a judgment call that leaders and their teams make dozens of times per day.

My decision to hire experts rather than build an AI agent was this kind of judgment call. The data might have suggested that an AI agent was more cost-effective. But my judgment said that for this particular project, with this particular client, human expertise would create more value. I was right, but I couldn't have proven it in advance. That's what makes it a leadership decision.

A Framework for AI-Augmented Decisions

When facing a decision where AI provides one recommendation but your intuition suggests another path, work through these steps:

1. Consult the Algorithm

What does the data suggest? What patterns has the AI identified? Don't dismiss it. AI often sees things we miss. Understand its recommendation fully.

2. Consult Your Values

What outcome aligns with who you want to be as an organization? What serves your vision? Values aren't constraints on decisions. They're the foundation of them.

3. Consult Affected Stakeholders

Who will be impacted, and what would they want you to consider? Often the people closest to the consequences have insights you lack.

4. Consult Your Intuition

What does your experience and judgment tell you, even if you can't fully articulate why? Intuition is pattern recognition built from experience. It's valuable even when it can't be explained.

5. Make the Call

Synthesize all inputs, but accept that ultimately a human must decide and be accountable. Don't hide behind *"the algorithm said so."* You chose to deploy the algorithm. You chose to follow or override it. Own that.

6. Learn from the Outcome

Whatever happens, extract lessons to improve future decisions. If you overrode the AI and were right, what did you see that it missed? If you were wrong, what should you have weighted differently?

The key insight is that good leadership doesn't mean always trusting the algorithm or always overriding it. It means developing the judgment to know which moments require which approach.

Looking at our value equation: this is where human judgment directly multiplies (or divides) AI utility. Poor judgment wastes high AI capability. Strong judgment amplifies it exponentially.

Preventing Atrophy: Keeping Teams Human

This deserves its own section because it's the leadership challenge most leaders miss entirely.

We discussed in Chapter 4 the risk of cognitive atrophy when people outsource their thinking to AI. As a leader, you have special responsibility to prevent this in your organization.

Warning Signs of Organizational Atrophy

People produce more but think less. Output increases but insight declines. Documents get longer but add less value.

Nobody can explain the reasoning. When you ask *"why did we recommend this?"* the answer is *"the AI suggested it"* rather than *"here's the strategic logic."*

Quality failures aren't caught. Errors that should be obvious slip through because people trust AI output without reviewing it critically.

Dependency grows. People become uncomfortable making decisions without AI input, even for straightforward situations that don't require it.

Innovation declines. Ideas become variations on what AI suggests rather than genuine breakthroughs that challenge assumptions.

If you're seeing these patterns, your organization is atrophying even as it appears more productive.

Practices to Prevent Atrophy

Mandate *"AI-free"* work. Regularly assign tasks that must be completed without AI assistance. This keeps cognitive muscles strong. Like athletes who train at high altitude to build capacity, your team needs to practice thinking without augmentation.

Require explanation, not just output. Before anything is shared with clients or stakeholders, the person who created it must be able to explain every key point in their own words and justify why it's right for this context.

Celebrate thoughtful work, not just fast work. When someone takes time to think deeply rather than defaulting to AI generation, recognize it publicly. This signals what you actually value.

Model healthy AI use. Share openly when you use AI and when you don't. Explain your reasoning. Show that using AI is a choice, not a default.

Create reflection practices. Regular team discussions about what you're learning, what AI is good and bad at, where you're becoming dependent, where you're maintaining independent judgment.

The goal isn't to reject AI. It's to ensure AI amplifies human capability rather than replaces it. That requires active, ongoing leadership attention.

Leading with Empathy and Ethics

Technical competence used to be enough for leadership. You rose to management because you were the best engineer, the best consultant, the best analyst. Your leadership came from expertise.

This model is breaking down because technical expertise is increasingly commoditized by AI. The differentiator for leaders is no longer what you know but how you lead.

Empathy as Strategic Advantage

When I spent time in those client meetings for the climate finance study, the experts I hired didn't just bring technical knowledge. They brought empathy, the ability to understand what the client was really asking for beneath the formal terms of reference.

One of them noticed during the inception call that the client's project manager asked many times questions about timelines for one deliverable. The project manager wasn't questioning our proposal. He was worried about whether his team could have the time to review the first draft just before holidays. Then we realised a milestone was being proposed at a time when the client would have not been as responsive as expected, this led us to restructure the schedule to be more implementable rather than just mechanically optimal.

AI can't do that. It can't read body language, interpret unspoken concerns, or sense what people are afraid to say out loud. These remain distinctly human capabilities that determine whether your work creates real value or sits unused on a shelf.

Empathy allows you to understand what people actually need rather than what they say they need, to navigate change with minimal resistance by acknowledging fears rather than dismissing them, to build loyalty in competitive markets where employees have options, and to spot problems before they explode by sensing tension before it shows up in metrics.

Ethics as North Star

Leaders set the ethical tone for entire organizations. This isn't about policy documents. It's about the choices you make when no one is watching and the principles you refuse to compromise even when it costs you.

Throughout this book, we've established that ethics isn't a constraint on value creation. Ethics IS value creation. It builds trust (perception), ensures sustainable impact, and guides judgment in ways that multiply long-term value even when they reduce short-term metrics.

As a leader, your ethical choices ripple through your organization. When I chose to hire experts rather than attempt an AI shortcut, I was signaling that we value genuine expertise over appearing cutting-edge. When I made that junior colleague's AI mistake a learning moment rather than a firing offense, I was signaling that growth matters more than perfection.

One powerful practice is the *"front page test."* Before any major decision, ask: *"If this appeared on the front page of the newspaper tomorrow, would I be proud or embarrassed?"* If the answer is embarrassed, reconsider the decision.

But go further: Would you be proud if your children read about this decision? Would you want other leaders in your industry to follow your example? These questions cut through rationalization and get to the heart of ethical leadership.

Leading Through Uncertainty: Strategies for the Fog

Perhaps the most challenging aspect of leadership in the AI age is navigating genuine uncertainty.

When I received that call saying I'd soon be irrelevant, I faced profound uncertainty. Should I double down on human expertise? Pivot to building AI tools? Try to do both? There was no playbook, no clear path, no guarantee any choice would work.

Leaders don't have the luxury of waiting for clarity. You must make decisions and move forward despite uncertainty.

Five Strategies for Leading in Fog

1. Scenario Planning

Don't predict the future. Prepare for multiple futures. What if AI progress accelerates? Plateaus? Faces regulatory restrictions? What if your industry is disrupted? What if it isn't?

Have plans for each. Then watch indicators to see which future is emerging and adapt accordingly.

2. Portfolio Approach

Don't bet everything on one strategy. When I faced that decision about the climate finance study, I didn't choose *"only human experts"* or *"only AI."* I chose a hybrid approach that I could adjust based on what I learned.

Maintain multiple bets: some conservative (continuing what works), some experimental (trying new approaches), some defensive (preparing for threats), some offensive (pursuing opportunities).

3. Fast Feedback Loops

When you can't predict, you must learn quickly. Build systems that give you rapid feedback on what's working.

For me, this meant staying in close contact with clients, asking explicitly what value they were receiving, tracking not just project completion but long-term impact and repeat business.

4. Reversible Decisions

When possible, make decisions that can be reversed if you learn they were wrong. Hiring experts was reversible. If it hadn't worked, I could pivot to different approaches. Building a large AI development team would have been harder to reverse.

Delay irreversible commitments (major technology investments, fundamental business model changes, large layoffs) until you have better information.

5. Transparency About Uncertainty

Don't pretend to have all the answers. Being honest about what you don't know builds trust more than false confidence.

I've been transparent with my team about the challenges we face, the questions I'm wrestling with, the experiments we're running. This creates psychological safety (if the leader admits uncertainty, so can I) and collaborative problem-solving (everyone contributes ideas rather than waiting for the leader to have answers).

The Leader's Inner Work: Facing Your Own Irrelevance

All of this outward-facing leadership work rests on a foundation of inner work:

the leader's own relationship with AI, change, and uncertainty.

When my client told me I'd soon be irrelevant, I had to grapple with fundamental questions about my identity. If AI can do what I do, who am I? What value do I actually bring? Is my career over?

These aren't just practical questions. They're existential ones. And every leader in the AI age must face them.

Identity: If much of what made you successful is becoming automated, who are you as a leader? What core value do you bring that remains irreplaceable?

For me, the answer emerged through that climate finance project. My irreplaceable value isn't technical analysis (AI can do that). It's judgment about what kind of expertise a situation requires, about how to combine different capabilities, about what clients really need beyond what they ask for, and about how to create trust and lasting relationships.

Fear: The anxiety about irrelevance, about making wrong decisions, about leading people into an uncertain future. This fear is real and must be acknowledged rather than suppressed.

I was genuinely afraid when I got that call. Afraid I'd made the wrong career choices. Afraid I was too old to adapt. Afraid my company would fail. Acknowledging that fear rather than denying it allowed me to work through it constructively.

Adaptation: Your own willingness to learn, to be a beginner again, to admit ignorance and ask for help.

I've had to learn new tools, new ways of working, new business models. At times, I've felt incompetent. The experts I hired know things I don't. That's uncomfortable but necessary.

The leaders who navigate this era successfully aren't those without fear or doubt. They're those who face fear and doubt honestly, do their inner work, and show up anyway.

This is the essence of courage: not the absence of fear, but action in the presence of fear.

The Through Line: Leadership as Human Work

Everything in this chapter points to a single insight: leadership in the AI age is fundamentally about being more human, not less.

As technical skills become commoditized, leadership becomes about the irreducibly human work of creating vision, building culture, exercising judgment, showing empathy, holding ethics, preventing atrophy, and navigating uncertainty with courage.

Looking at our value equation one final time:

Value = [(AI Utility × Human Judgment) × Perception] + Impact

Leaders shape every element. You decide what AI utility to deploy. You cultivate human judgment in yourself and your team. You build perception through transparency, empathy, and ethical consistency. You ensure impact serves human flourishing.

This isn't just about business success. It's about preserving human agency and dignity in an age of intelligent machines. It's about ensuring that as our tools become more powerful, we become more human rather than more mechanical.

As we move to the next chapter on entrepreneurship, remember that leadership isn't just for people with CEO titles. Anyone who influences others, who builds things, who makes choices that affect more than themselves is engaged in leadership.

The question is only whether you'll lead consciously and courageously, or drift through the transformation hoping someone else will figure it out.

The future needs leaders who can orchestrate human and machine capabilities to create value neither could create alone. Leaders who prevent atrophy while enabling augmentation. Leaders who face their own irrelevance and emerge with clarity about their irreplaceable contribution.

That's the work. And it's more important now than ever.

After Efficiency

Chapter 9

The Entrepreneurial Mindset

I decided to found Climate Platform during the COVID pandemic. My previous work required extensive travel, and at a critical moment when it wasn't safe to do so, my boss asked me to travel anyway. That request triggered something fundamental in me: a reconsideration of whether I wanted to continue spending my life serving loyally people who could put my life at risk for business convenience.

At the time, AI was already being used by corporations like Google and Facebook, giving them the edge to become the multi-billion-dollar conglomerates they are today. But it wasn't democratically spread as it is now. The tools that make solo consulting viable today simply didn't exist yet, or were prohibitively expensive.

Moving from the security of a monthly salary to the uncertainty of consulting life was not an easy step. Many times I asked myself: *"What if I don't have clients?" "What if my services are no longer needed?"* At the same time, I knew I had skills and experience that were valuable to the market at that time. Or so I thought.

I lost the first tender I applied for. It created huge anxiety. But the potential client had a transparent system in place, and I was informed we came second. Despite the anxiety, I knew if we could come second, we could also win a tender. I kept moving.

I adjusted my fees. Because I had a very high impression of my value before that tender, but the market was not ready to reward me yet at the level I thought

I was worth. That was a humbling lesson: your value isn't what you think you're worth. It's what the market will actually pay, and you have to earn that through demonstrated impact, not assumed expertise.

After some years of practice, natural language processing was no longer a thing in textbooks. Where before the big innovation was seeing a computer take notes while I spoke my expertise, now the computer could generate text on its own. Everything was changing again. And I had to ask myself the same questions: *"Am I still relevant?" "Can I still create value?" "What if AI makes me obsolete?"*

This chapter isn't about how to become the next tech unicorn. It's about cultivating the entrepreneurial mindset that spots opportunities, takes intelligent risks, and creates value in spaces others overlook. It's about the reality of entrepreneurship in the AI age, with all its fears, failures, and hard-won lessons.

Entrepreneurship as Value Creation, Not Just Company Building

Before we dive into identifying opportunities or building businesses, let's be clear about what entrepreneurship actually means in the AI age.

The entrepreneurial mindset isn't only for people starting companies. It's a way of approaching any work or problem with agency, creativity, and a willingness to take intelligent risks.

Looking at our value equation from Chapter 3:

Value = [(AI Utility × Human Judgment) × Perception] + Impact

Entrepreneurs orchestrate all elements of this equation. They decide what AI capabilities to deploy, they apply judgment to ensure those capabilities serve real needs, they build perception through trust and demonstrated results, and they ensure the work creates positive impact.

Whether you're starting a company, innovating within an organization, or building a sustainable practice like Climate Platform, you're engaged in entrepreneurial value creation.

Three Paths of Entrepreneurship

Traditional Entrepreneurship: Building Companies

Creating organizations designed to scale, often with external investment, employees, and growth targets. This is the venture-backed startup path that gets most media attention but represents a small fraction of entrepreneurial activity.

Intrapreneurship: Innovation Within Organizations

Some of the most impactful innovation happens within existing companies by people who think like entrepreneurs. Spotting opportunities others miss. Taking initiative without waiting for permission. Building coalitions to support new ideas. Experimenting rapidly and learning from failures. Creating value in ways that weren't in anyone's job description.

Lifestyle Entrepreneurship: Building Sustainable Practices

Creating businesses that support meaningful lives while solving real problems. This is the path I chose with Climate Platform. Not trying to build the next unicorn, but building something sustainable that creates genuine value while allowing me to live according to my values.

AI makes this path more accessible by reducing the overhead needed to run a business. One person with good AI augmentation can do work that previously required a team. This creates opportunity for specialized consultants, content creators, and service providers that were previously unviable.

All three paths are valid. All three create value. The question isn't which is *"better,"* but which aligns with your purpose, constraints, and vision for your life.

Identifying Unmet Needs in a Changing Landscape

The AI revolution creates two simultaneous dynamics:

Displacement: Tasks that humans used to do are now automated, threatening existing business models and jobs.

Creation: New problems emerge that didn't exist before, and existing problems become solvable in ways that weren't possible previously.

Entrepreneurs with an AI-age mindset focus less on the displacement (which is crowded and often demoralizing) and more on the creation (which is abundant with opportunity).

Where I Found My Opportunity

When I started Climate Platform, I wasn't thinking about AI at all. I was thinking about a gap I'd observed through years of working in climate finance: mid-sized institutions and governments in emerging economies needed sophisticated climate finance strategies, but existing consulting firms were either too expensive for their budgets or too generic in their approach.

The big consulting firms would send junior staff with templates. I could bring senior expertise with contextual understanding. I knew the regulatory frameworks, the funding mechanisms, the political dynamics. More importantly, I understood the human side: the climate officers feeling overwhelmed, the finance ministers facing pressure from multiple stakeholders, the communities whose futures depended on getting this right.

That gap, that need for sophisticated expertise delivered with genuine understanding and at reasonable cost, that was my entrepreneurial opportunity. AI came later, as a tool to augment what I could deliver, not as the core value proposition.

This is crucial: start with the human need, not with the technology.

Six Spaces Where Opportunities Hide

Through my experience and observation, I've identified six categories where entrepreneurial opportunities consistently emerge in the AI age:

1. The Gaps Left by Automation

When AI automates one part of a workflow, it often creates bottlenecks or gaps elsewhere in the process.

In my work, AI tools can now generate draft climate finance proposals quickly. But someone still needs to ensure those proposals align with specific country contexts, navigate political sensitivities, address implementation realities, and build trust with stakeholders. I provide that layer.

2. The Human Interpretation Layer

AI generates outputs, but humans still need to interpret, validate, and apply them contextually.

When I deliver climate finance studies, the data and analysis might be AI-augmented, but the strategic recommendations require understanding things AI can't grasp: the capacity constraints of the implementing agency, the political dynamics that will affect adoption, the cultural factors that shape how solutions will be received.

3. The Ethics and Governance Space

As AI becomes more powerful and pervasive, organizations need help navigating ethical, legal, and governance challenges. Companies using AI for hiring need auditing services. Organizations deploying AI need frameworks for responsible use. This is a growth sector.

4. The Education and Change Management Need

Individuals and organizations want to leverage AI but don't know where to start. Corporate training programs teaching teams how to effectively use AI tools, integrate them into workflows, and maintain quality while increasing efficiency are booming.

5. The Human Connection Premium

As automation increases, people increasingly value authentic human connection in certain domains. In my work, clients could theoretically get generic climate advice from AI-generated reports. But they hire me because they want someone who understands their specific context, who they can trust, who will stay engaged through the implementation challenges.

6. The Customization Gap

Generic AI tools serve broad needs reasonably well. But specific industries, use cases, or communities often need tailored solutions. Climate Platform exists in this gap: specialized enough to truly understand climate finance in emerging economies, but accessible enough to serve clients the big firms ignore.

Value Mapping: Starting with Need, Not Technology

The biggest mistake aspiring entrepreneurs make is building something they think is cool rather than something customers actually need.

The AI age amplifies this mistake because it's so easy to build things now. You can create a functional prototype in days. But just because you can build it doesn't mean anyone wants it.

My Value Mapping Process

1. Start with the Customer, Not the Technology

When I started Climate Platform, I didn't begin with *"What AI tools can I use?"* I began with *"What do climate officers at mid-sized institutions struggle with?"*

Through years of working in the field, I knew the pain points viscerally: Documentation requirements from multiple frameworks. Keeping up with regulatory changes. Translating technical data into board-friendly narratives. Accessing funding mechanisms. Building credible proposals with limited staff.

Once I understood these pain points deeply, then I explored how various tools (including but not limited to AI) could help address them.

2. Validate Pain Before Building Solutions

Before I officially launched Climate Platform, I had conversations. Lots of conversations. Not pitching services, but asking questions:

"Walk me through the last time you tried to access climate finance. What worked? What didn't? How much time did it cost you? What would you pay to solve this?"

These specific, story-based questions revealed whether the pain was real and acute enough that people would actually pay to solve it. Some pain points I thought were significant turned out to be minor annoyances. Others I'd underestimated were major obstacles consuming enormous time and resources.

3. Map the Value Chain

For any solution, you need to understand:

- Who experiences the pain point?
- Who makes the decision to hire you?

- Who works with you day-to-day?
- Who benefits from the results?

These are often different people, and you need to create value for all of them.

In my work, the climate officer experiences the pain, the finance minister or executive director makes the hiring decision, the technical staff work with me daily, and ultimately the communities and ecosystems benefit from successful climate finance mobilization.

If I only focused on making the climate officer's job easier without considering what the finance minister cares about (political feasibility, budget constraints) or what communities need (genuine impact, not just documentation), I'd fail to create sustainable value.

4. Understand the Jobs-to-be-Done

People don't want your product or service. They want progress in their lives.

Clayton Christensen's *"Jobs-to-be-Done"* framework asks: What job is the customer hiring your product to do?

When an International Agency hires Climate Platform, they're not just hiring *"climate finance consulting."* They're hiring us to help them demonstrate to international funders that they're serious about climate action, to position themselves as credible vehicle of climate finance to the recipients, to navigate complex requirements they don't have capacity to handle internally, and ultimately to access resources that will help their member countrics adapt to climate impacts.

Understanding the deeper job, not just the surface request, is what allows you to create genuine value rather than just deliver a commodity service.

The Reality of Starting: Fear, Failure, and Forward Motion

Let me be honest about what entrepreneurship actually feels like, because the sanitized success stories you read online miss the texture of the experience.

The Fear is Real

When I lost that first tender, the anxiety was overwhelming. Not just disappointment, but existential fear. *"Maybe I'm not as valuable as I thought.*

Maybe I can't actually do this. Maybe I should have stayed in the secure job even if it meant compromising my values."

Every entrepreneur I know, including wildly successful ones, lives with some version of this fear. Fear of failure. Fear of looking foolish. Fear of wasting time or money. Fear of discovering you're not as capable as you hoped.

The difference isn't that successful entrepreneurs lack fear. It's that they act despite it. They treat fear as data, not destiny. It tells you something matters to you. It signals you're taking a real risk, not a pretend one. But it doesn't get a veto on whether you move forward.

Adjusting My Value Proposition

After losing that first tender, I had to confront an uncomfortable truth: my perception of my value didn't match the market's perception of my value. I thought my years of experience and expertise commanded premium rates. The market disagreed.

I had two choices: insist on my rates and hope someone eventually agreed, or adjust my pricing to match market reality while I built reputation and demonstrated results.

I chose the latter. It was humbling. But it was also strategic. By pricing accessibly while delivering exceptional value, I built a portfolio of successful projects, client testimonials, and word-of-mouth referrals that eventually allowed me to command higher rates, not based on my assumed value but on my proven impact.

Looking at our three dimensions of value: I had decent utility (I could do the work), but low perception (the market didn't know or trust me yet), which meant my impact was limited because I couldn't get hired. By adjusting pricing to match perception while consistently delivering high utility and impact, I gradually built perception until all three dimensions aligned.

The Pivotal Choice: People or Technology

When I was hired for that climate finance study I mentioned in Chapter 8, I faced a defining moment. I could try to do the entire project myself using AI tools to augment my work. This would maximize my profit margin and prove I could compete in the AI age.

Or I could hire two experts whose skills complemented mine. This would reduce my margin but might create better outcomes.

I chose people. And looking back, it was one of the best decisions I've made.

Those experts brought insights I simply couldn't have generated, even with the best AI tools. They asked questions from their unique perspectives that improved the entire project. The client was so satisfied they extended our contract and recommended us to another firm.

Me alone with AI tools would have produced adequate work. Our team, each person using AI to augment their unique expertise, produced exceptional work.

This taught me something fundamental about entrepreneurship in the AI age: the question isn't whether to use AI or hire people. It's how to orchestrate human and AI capabilities to create value neither could create alone.

That's the essence of the entrepreneurial mindset: seeing opportunities for value creation that others miss, then orchestrating resources (human, technological, financial) to realize those opportunities.

Small Bets, Not Big Leaps

The romanticized version of entrepreneurship involves quitting your job, maxing out credit cards, and going all in. This makes for good movies but terrible strategy.

Smart entrepreneurs make small, reversible bets. They test ideas while maintaining financial security. They validate demand before building supply. They learn fast and cheap before committing large resources.

AI makes this easier than ever. You can test business concepts with minimal upfront investment. You can build prototypes in days. You can reach potential customers globally without an office or staff.

My Small Bets Approach

I didn't quit my job and immediately start a consulting firm. I took on small projects while still employed, testing whether I could deliver value independently. When those succeeded, I took slightly bigger bets. Only after accumulating evidence that Climate Platform could work did I fully commit.

Even then, I didn't immediately hire staff or rent office space. I stayed lean. And by the way, 100% of my turnover comes from clients who never visited my office. This allowed me to be profitable from early on rather than burning through savings while *"scaling."*

For most readers, this is the realistic path: not venture-backed unicorns, but sustainable practices built through intelligent experimentation and gradual growth.

The Compound Effect of Starting

Here's what happens when you actually begin, even imperfectly:

You learn faster than people who are still planning. Every conversation, every test, every small failure teaches you something. You accumulate knowledge that no amount of research could provide. My understanding of what clients actually need came from doing projects, not from market research reports.

You build a network. The people you talk to introduce you to others. Your initial customers become advocates. Mentors appear when you're actually doing something, not just thinking about it. Most of my clients came through referrals from previous satisfied clients.

You develop entrepreneurial muscle. The first time you pitch a potential client, it's terrifying. The tenth time, it's routine. The confidence you build from taking action compounds over time. I'm still nervous before big pitches, but I've learned to act despite nervousness rather than waiting for it to disappear.

You create luck. Opportunities emerge not because you're lucky but because you're in motion. The person who's actively building something is visible. The person still preparing in private is invisible. That contract extension I mentioned? That happened because we were visible, engaged, and delivering value. Luck rewards action.

Three Principles for AI-Age Entrepreneurs

Based on my experience and observation, three principles guide successful entrepreneurship in the AI age:

1. Purpose as Competitive Advantage

Why did I choose climate finance? Not just because it's important (though it is), but because I genuinely care about the outcomes. That care shows up in how I work, the extra effort I invest, the relationships I build.

In a world where technical capabilities are increasingly commoditized, purpose becomes a differentiator. Clients sense whether you're just doing a job or whether you're genuinely invested in their success. That perception shapes trust, which shapes long-term relationships, which shapes sustainable business success.

Your purpose doesn't have to be saving the world. It can be helping small businesses thrive, making technology accessible, creating beautiful things, or solving puzzles that fascinate you. But it should be genuine, because authenticity can't be faked long-term, and inauthenticity eventually undermines all three dimensions of value.

2. Build Reputation, Not Just Revenue

When I lost that first tender, I could have seen it as pure failure. Instead, I saw it as valuable feedback and an opportunity to learn. When I adjusted my pricing, I wasn't just trying to win contracts. I was investing in reputation.

Every project is an opportunity not just to earn fees but to demonstrate value, build trust, generate testimonials, and earn referrals. This long-term orientation means sometimes accepting lower-margin work that builds capabilities or relationships that will pay off later.

In the AI age, where technical barriers to entry are low and competition is intense, reputation is your moat. Spend years building it, and clients come to you. Neglect it for short-term gains, and you're constantly hustling for the next gig.

3. Stay Agile, Stay Human

AI is evolving rapidly. New capabilities emerge constantly. Business models that work today may be obsolete tomorrow. The entrepreneurs who thrive are those who stay agile, continuously learning, adapting, and experimenting.

But agility doesn't mean abandoning your humanity. It means using AI to amplify your human capabilities, not replace them. It means maintaining judgment even as you deploy automation. It means building genuine relationships even as you scale through technology.

When that client called to warn me about AI making me irrelevant, I could have panicked and tried to become a technology company. Instead, I asked: *"What's my irreplaceable human contribution?"* The answer was judgment, contextual understanding, relationship building, and ethical commitment to impact. I've doubled down on those while using AI to handle what it does well.

Your First Step Tomorrow

Don't wait to finish this book. Don't wait until you have more time, more skills, or more clarity.

Tomorrow, have one conversation with someone who might have a problem you could solve. That's it. One conversation. Not to sell anything. Just to understand.

Ask them about their struggles, their workarounds, their frustrations. Listen for the emotional weight behind their words. One of those conversations will surprise you. Someone will say something that shifts your entire perspective. That's where the real opportunity lives, in that surprise.

Then build the smallest possible thing that tests whether your surprise was meaningful. Not a product. A test. Maybe it's offering to help manually with their problem. Maybe it's creating a simple tool. Maybe it's writing an article about the issue and seeing who responds.

The goal isn't to prove you're right. The goal is to learn fast and cheap whether you're wrong.

The Courage to Begin

Entrepreneurship isn't about certainty. It's about curiosity and a tolerance for discomfort. It's about beginning before you're ready, learning as you go, and adjusting course constantly.

In the AI age, this matters more than ever because waiting for certainty means waiting forever. Technology evolves too quickly. Market conditions shift too rapidly. The information you need to make a perfect decision will never arrive.

The entrepreneurial mindset isn't something you have or don't have. It's something you develop through practice. And practice starts with courage, the courage to begin despite fear, to act despite uncertainty, to create value in a world that's changing faster than any of us can fully comprehend.

I started Climate Platform in a pandemic, at a moment of personal and global crisis, with no guarantee it would work. It has worked, not because I had special insight or advantages, but because I was willing to begin, to learn from failure, to adjust course, and to keep moving forward.

You have that same capacity. The question is whether you'll use it.

As we move to Part IV, we'll explore a comprehensive framework for integrating everything we've discussed: value creation, human contribution, ethics, leadership, and entrepreneurship into a coherent approach to thriving in the AI age.

But frameworks without action remain theory. The most important thing you can do isn't read the next chapter. It's have that first conversation, make that first small bet, take that first step toward creating value in the world.

Everything else follows from the courage to begin.

PART IV
A Framework for the Future

Chapter 10

The V.A.L.U.E. Framework

Throughout this book, we've explored value from multiple angles: its evolving definition, the unique human contribution in an AI world, the ethical imperatives, and the practical work of creating products, leading teams, and building ventures.

Now it's time to integrate these insights into a coherent framework you can apply immediately, whether you're an individual professional, a team leader, or an organization builder.

I call it the V.A.L.U.E. Framework: five interconnected principles that guide sustainable value creation in the age of artificial intelligence.

V - Vision: Clarity in a Complex World

The Principle: Vision is your North Star. It's the answer to *"What are we here to create?"* and *"Who do we serve?"* When technology changes daily and strategies must adapt constantly, vision provides the stable reference point.

Why It Matters in the AI Age:

AI excels at optimization but has no conception of purpose. It can tell you the most efficient path to a goal, but it can't tell you which goals are worth pursuing. That's the work of vision.

Without clear vision, organizations and individuals get swept along by technological possibility, building things because they can rather than because they should. Vision acts as a filter, helping you distinguish between opportunities that align with your purpose and distractions that don't.

Vision in Practice:

Strong vision answers three questions:

1. What change do we want to see in the world? Not what product we'll build or what market we'll serve, but what transformation we're working toward. Patagonia's vision isn't *"make great outdoor gear."* It's *"We're in business to save our home planet."*

2. **Who do we serve, and how will their lives be better? Specific enough to guide decisions, broad enough to allow flexibility in how you serve. A healthcare company might say:** *"We serve people managing chronic illness, and we want to help them live fuller lives with less fear and friction."*

3. What won't we compromise? The values and principles that define how you work, even when they're costly. These boundaries keep you from drifting when pressure mounts.

Vision is seeing what could be, not just what is. It's the ability to look at the current reality and imagine a better alternative.

But vision in the AI age requires a new kind of clarity. You're not just imagining better products or more efficient systems. You're imagining how human and machine capabilities can combine to serve needs that neither could address alone.

What Clear Vision Looks Like

Bad vision statements are vague and aspirational: *"We want to change the world." "We're disrupting the industry." "We're leveraging AI to transform X."*

These sound impressive but provide no actual direction. They're fog dressed up as clarity.

Clear vision answers three specific questions:

Who are we serving? Not demographics. Actual humans with actual struggles. *"Small business owners drowning in administrative work"* is clearer than *"the SMB market."*

What transformation are we enabling? What does their life look like after engaging with what you build? *"They reclaim ten hours per week to focus on their craft instead of paperwork"* is clearer than *"increased productivity."*

Why does this matter? What larger purpose does this serve? *"Because everyone deserves to spend their limited time on work that matters to them"* connects to something deeper than profit.

Notice what's missing: technology. Clear vision focuses on human outcomes, not technical means. The AI tools you use might change next year. The transformation you're enabling shouldn't.

Testing Your Vision

Can you explain it to someone outside your field in under thirty seconds and have them understand not just what you do but why it matters?

Does it get you out of bed on the hard days? Vision isn't just external messaging. It's internal fuel. If your vision doesn't move you, it won't move anyone else.

Does it guide decisions? When you face a choice between two options, does your vision make the right path obvious? If not, your vision isn't clear enough.

Living Into Your Vision

Vision isn't a one-time declaration. It's a living orientation that you return to constantly.

Revisit it quarterly. Has your understanding deepened? Has the landscape shifted in ways that require adaptation? Are you still serving the same transformation, or has your focus drifted?

Share it relentlessly. Every conversation, every email, every meeting is a chance to reinforce what you're working toward and why. People can't align with a vision they don't know or understand.

Measure against it. When evaluating success, ask not just *"Did we hit our numbers?"* but *"Did we move closer to the transformation we envision?"*

A - Augmentation: Partnering with AI

The debate about *"humans versus AI"* is irrelevant. The real question is: How do we combine human and artificial intelligence to create value neither could create alone?

Those who resist AI entirely will be outpaced by those who embrace it. Those who blindly adopt AI without maintaining human judgment will build fast, fragile systems that eventually fail or cause harm. The sweet spot is thoughtful augmentation.Augmentation means using AI to amplify your capabilities, not replace them. It's the difference between competing with machines and collaborating with them.

Most people approach AI in one of two broken ways:

Some ignore it, hoping to preserve their current approach unchanged. This is denial, and it leads to obsolescence.

Others surrender to it, letting algorithms make decisions and outsourcing judgment. This is abdication, and it leads to losing the very skills that make you valuable.

Augmentation is the third path. You remain in the driver's seat, but you use AI to see farther, move faster, and accomplish more than you could alone.

The Augmentation Mindset in Practice

Start by mapping your work into three categories:

Tasks AI handles better than you. Data processing, pattern recognition across large datasets, generating variations and options, consistency across repetitive work. Let AI own these.

Tasks you handle better than AI. Judgment in ambiguous situations, emotional intelligence, ethical reasoning, building trust, creative leaps to entirely new domains. Keep these firmly in your control.

Tasks neither handles well alone but together you excel at. Strategic analysis (AI surfaces patterns, you interpret significance), content creation (AI generates drafts, you refine with voice and judgment), problem-solving (AI suggests approaches, you choose based on context).

The power is in the third category. This is where augmentation creates value neither human nor machine could generate independently.

Practical Augmentation Strategies

Use AI as a thinking partner. When stuck on a problem, explain it to an AI. The act of articulation often clarifies your own thinking. The AI's response might not be the answer, but it can spark a direction you hadn't considered.

Let AI handle first drafts. Writing, analysis, design. Whatever your domain, use AI to generate initial options quickly. Then apply your judgment to refine, personalize, and elevate.

Automate the routine to focus on the exceptional. Every hour you spend on routine tasks is an hour you're not spending on high-value work that only you can do. Ruthlessly automate anything that doesn't require your unique capabilities.

Build feedback loops. AI learns from your corrections and preferences. The more you work with it, the better it gets at augmenting your specific style and needs. This compounds over time.

Avoiding Augmentation Pitfalls:

Augmentation only works if you continue developing your human capabilities. If you outsource all your writing to AI, your ability to write atrophies. If you let algorithms make all your decisions, your judgment weakens.

Use AI to handle the routine so you can practice the exceptional. Use it to save time so you can invest that time in deepening your expertise, not just producing more output.

The goal isn't efficiency for its own sake. It's creating space for the work only you can do. The following pittfalls must be avoided :

- **Over-reliance**: Using AI for everything and atrophying human skills. Maintain practices where you exercise judgment without AI assist.

- **Under-utilization**: Rejecting AI from fear or stubbornness and falling behind competitors who embrace it.

- **Black-box acceptance**: Trusting AI outputs without understanding how they're generated. Always maintain the ability to interrogate the logic.

- **Capability mismatch**: Using AI for tasks it's not suited for (like ethical decisions) or keeping humans on tasks AI handles better (like processing huge datasets).

L - Love: Serving Real Human Needs

Love is not a word we use comfortably in business contexts. It sounds soft, impractical, naive.

But here's what I mean by love in the context of value creation: genuine care about the people you serve. Not as market segments or user personas or revenue sources. As actual humans whose lives you want to improve.

This isn't sentimentality. It's the most practical foundation for sustainable value creation.

Why Love Matters Economically

When you genuinely care about the people you serve, several things happen:

You notice needs others miss. You're not just looking at data. You're paying attention to struggles, frustrations, and unspoken hopes. This gives you insights no market research report could provide.

You make better decisions under uncertainty. When you can't predict the outcome, you ask: *"What would be best for the people we serve?"* This compass points true even when everything else is ambiguous.

You build loyalty that transcends price. People feel the difference between a company that sees them as revenue and one that sees them as humans worthy of care. That feeling creates attachment stronger than any loyalty program.

You attract talent that shares your values. The best people want to work on something meaningful. When they see genuine care for customers or communities, they want to be part of that.

What Love Looks Like in Practice

It's the product team that says *"We could add this feature and increase revenue, but it would make the product more confusing for our least tech-savvy users. Let's find another way."*

It's the customer service rep who spends an extra thirty minutes helping someone even though it tanks their efficiency metrics.

It's the founder who turns down a lucrative contract because the client wants to use the product in ways that would harm end users.

It's thousands of small choices, invisible to outsiders, where you prioritize what's right for the humans you serve over what's expedient for you.

The Hard Part About Love

Love is expensive in the short term. It's slower than exploitation. It requires saying no to opportunities that would compromise your integrity. It means accepting lower margins to maintain accessibility. It demands patience when quick wins are available.

But love compounds. Every choice made from genuine care builds trust. Every customer well-served becomes an advocate. Every team member who sees you prioritize human wellbeing over profit becomes more committed.

Five years from now, the company built on love looks completely different from the company built on extraction. One has deep roots and loyal community. The other has churn and constant need for new acquisition.

Checking Your Orientation

Ask yourself honestly: Do you celebrate when someone finds success with your offering, or only when they pay you more? Do you feel protective of your customers' interests, or do you see them primarily as a means to your goals?

Do you design for their actual needs, or for your desired metrics? When they struggle, do you feel genuine concern or just frustration at a support ticket?

These aren't judgment questions. We all drift toward using people rather than serving them. The key is catching yourself, recalibrating, and choosing love even when it costs something.

U - Uniqueness: Differentiating Meaningfully

In a world where AI can replicate most skills and knowledge, being *"good at your job"* isn't enough. Being the best in a traditional sense isn't even enough, because there's an AI that can match or exceed you in technical capability.

Your value increasingly comes from what makes you unreplicable. Not just different, but meaningfully unique in ways that matter to the people you serve.

The Wrong Kind of Differentiation

Many people try to differentiate through credentials, speed, or price. *"I have more degrees." "I'm faster." "I'm cheaper."*

These are temporary advantages at best. Someone else will get more credentials. AI will be faster. Someone desperate will be cheaper.

The Right Kind of Differentiation

Meaningful uniqueness comes from the intersection of three elements:

Your distinctive perspective. What do you see that others miss? What experiences have you had that shape how you understand problems? Your particular combination of background, culture, successes, and failures creates a lens no one else has.

Your specific values. What do you refuse to compromise on? What trade-offs are you unwilling to make? Your ethical commitments and priorities create boundaries that define your approach.

Your particular strengths. Not just what you're good at, but what you're good at that you also care about and that others need. The sweet spot where capability, passion, and value to others intersect.

These three elements combine to create something genuinely unique. Not because any single element is rare, but because your particular combination is unrepeatable.

Finding Your Unique Contribution

This isn't something you invent through clever positioning. It's something you discover through honest self-examination and conversation with people who know you.

Ask people who've worked with you: What do I bring that others don't? What do you come to me for that you wouldn't go to someone else for? When am I at my best?

Their answers will surprise you. The things that feel effortless to you, that you assume everyone can do, are often your unique strengths.

Then ask yourself: What problems do I care about more than most people do? What injustices make me angry? What possibilities excite me?

Your unique contribution lives where your natural strengths meet your deepest cares and other people's real needs.

Leaning Into Uniqueness

Once you identify what makes you unique, resist the urge to round off your edges. Don't try to be all things to all people. Don't soften your perspective to be more broadly acceptable.

The people who need exactly what you offer will find you if you're clear about what that is. The people who need something else will go elsewhere, and that's fine.

Your goal isn't maximum reach. It's maximum impact with the people you're meant to serve.

E - Ethics: Doing What Lasts

We covered ethics in depth in Chapter 6, but it deserves emphasis here because it's the foundation that holds the entire framework together.

Without ethics, vision becomes manipulation. Augmentation becomes exploitation. Love becomes sentimentality. Uniqueness becomes arrogance.

Ethics is what ensures that the value you create is genuine and sustainable, not just a clever extraction scheme dressed up in appealing language.

Ethics as Competitive Advantage

Here's what most people miss: ethics isn't a constraint on value creation. It's the source of enduring value.

Short-term thinking says *"Cut corners to move faster."* Ethical thinking says *"Build it right because we'll be living with the consequences for years."*

Short-term thinking says *"Exploit information asymmetry while you can."* Ethical thinking says *"Be transparent because trust compounds over time."*

Short-term thinking says *"Optimize for this quarter's numbers."* Ethical thinking says *"Make choices we'll be proud of in ten years."*

In the AI age, ethical behavior isn't just morally right. It's strategically essential. As technology enables ever more powerful interventions, the potential for harm scales exponentially. The organizations that survive and thrive will be those that chose to constrain their own power in service of human flourishing.

Your Ethical Foundation

Ethics isn't something you figure out once and then execute. It's a continuous practice of:

Pausing before acting. Not every decision that's legal or profitable is right. Build in space to ask *"Should we?"* before *"Can we?"*

Seeking diverse perspectives. Your blind spots are by definition invisible to you. Actively seek people who will challenge your thinking, especially when you're confident you're right.

Accepting accountability. When harm occurs, even unintentionally, own it. Apologize sincerely. Make amends. Learn. Don't hide behind complexity or blame the algorithm.

Choosing the harder right over the easier wrong. Ethics costs something, sometimes a lot. That's how you know it's real. If every ethical choice is convenient, you're probably not facing genuine dilemmas.

The Framework as a Whole

V.A.L.U.E. isn't a checklist. It's a set of lenses that work together:

Vision without ethics becomes harmful ambition. Augmentation without love becomes dehumanizing efficiency. Love without uniqueness becomes generic care. Uniqueness without vision becomes aimless differentiation. Ethics without augmentation becomes noble but ineffective effort.

Use all five elements together. Let them inform each other. When facing a decision, run it through each lens. If it fails any one test, reconsider.

This framework won't give you easy answers. It will give you better questions. And in a complex, rapidly changing world, better questions are more valuable than certain answers.

Chapter 11

Value Creation as a Lifestyle

Creating value isn't just what you do during work hours. It's not a role you step into and out of. It's a way of moving through the world, a set of principles that guide daily choices, and a practice that compounds over time.

This chapter is about making the frameworks we've explored operational in your actual life. Not as theory to admire, but as practices to implement. Not someday when you have more time or clarity, but starting tomorrow morning.

The V.A.L.U.E. Framework as Daily Practice

In Chapter 10, we introduced the V.A.L.U.E. Framework as a strategic tool. Now let's translate it into daily action.

Vision: Starting Each Day with Direction

Most people wake up and immediately react. Check phone. Respond to messages. Address urgencies. They're productive but not directed. Busy but not purposeful.

The Morning Practice (3 minutes):

Before checking your phone, ask three questions:

1. What value do I want to create today? Not a task list. A focus. *"Today I want to help my client see a path forward through their confusion." "Today I want*

to create work that reflects careful thinking, not just quick output." "Today I want to treat every person I encounter as worthy of full attention."

2. Where might I be tempted to compromise this vision? Anticipate the pressure points. *"The client will probably push for quick answers when what they need is thoughtful analysis." "My inbox will be full of urgent things that aren't important." "I'll want to use AI to finish quickly rather than think deeply first."*

3. What's one choice I can make today that aligns with my deeper purpose? Make it specific and achievable. Not *"be a better leader"* but *"have that difficult conversation with my team member."* Not *"create more value"* but *"spend an extra hour ensuring this deliverable is genuinely useful, not just complete."*

This practice keeps vision from being an abstract aspiration and makes it a concrete daily orientation.

Connecting to our three dimensions: Vision shapes what utility you pursue (not just any productivity, but meaningful work), how others perceive you (as purposeful rather than reactive), and ensures your impact is intentional rather than accidental.

Augmentation: Choosing Wisely Throughout the Day

We're living in the first era where the average person interacts with artificial intelligence dozens of times per day without even noticing. Your phone's keyboard predicts your next word. Your email filters spam. Your maps app routes you around traffic. Your music service queues your next song.

This ambient AI is designed to be invisible, to make your life easier without requiring you to think about it. And that's exactly the problem.

When AI becomes invisible, so do your choices. You stop noticing that you're being guided, optimized, predicted. You lose agency without realizing it.

The Practice of Conscious Augmentation:

Throughout your day, pause before delegating to AI and ask:

"What am I asking AI to do, and why?"

Are you using it to handle genuinely routine work (scheduling, formatting, data organization) so you can focus on judgment and creativity? Good augmentation.

Or are you using it to avoid thinking through a difficult problem, to skip the struggle that builds capability, to produce output without developing insight? That's atrophy disguised as efficiency.

"What am I keeping in my control?"

The core judgment, the creative vision, the ethical reasoning, the relationship building, these should remain human work that AI augments rather than replaces.

"Am I becoming more capable or more dependent?"

If you stopped using this AI tool tomorrow, would you be stronger from having used it (like an athlete who trains with tools that build capacity) or weaker (like someone whose muscles have atrophied from disuse)?

A Simple Daily Rule:

Do at least one significant piece of work each day without any AI assistance. Write a memo in your own words without checking suggestions. Solve a problem through your own reasoning before consulting AI. Have a conversation without checking your phone.

This isn't about rejecting AI. It's about ensuring you maintain the human capabilities that make AI augmentation valuable in the first place. Remember our value equation:

Value = [(AI Utility × Human Judgment) × Perception] + Impact. If human judgment goes to zero, the entire utility component collapses.

Connecting to dimensions: Augmentation directly shapes utility (how effectively you work), perception (whether people trust your outputs are genuinely yours), and impact (whether your work creates lasting value or just temporary efficiency).

Love: Serving Real Needs in Every Interaction

We discussed in Chapter 10 that *"love"* in a business context means genuinely serving people's wellbeing, not just their stated requests. But how do you actually practice this daily?

The Interaction Practice:

In each significant interaction, whether with clients, colleagues, or anyone else, pause to ask:

"What does this person actually need, not just what are they asking for?"

The client asks for a faster report. What they need is confidence that they're making the right decision with the information available.

The team member asks for clearer instructions. What they need is to feel trusted to use their judgment and supported when they're uncertain.

The family member asks if you're listening. What they need is to feel that they matter to you more than your phone does.

"What would genuine service look like here?"

Sometimes it means doing what they asked. Often it means something different: slowing down instead of speeding up, asking questions instead of providing answers, being present instead of being productive.

"Am I optimizing for efficiency or for impact?"

The efficient thing is often to give people what they literally requested and move on. The valuable thing is often to invest extra time understanding what would actually help them.

A Weekly Reflection:

Each Friday, identify one person you served genuinely this week. Not just provided a service to, but actually helped in a way that addressed their real need. Write down specifically what you noticed about their need and how you responded.

Then identify one interaction where you optimized for efficiency at the expense of service. What did you miss? What could you do differently next time?

This reflection builds the muscle of seeing beneath surface requests to genuine needs, which is perhaps the most valuable skill in the AI age.

Connecting to dimensions: Service orientation massively increases perception (people sense when you genuinely care about their wellbeing), often reduces short-term utility (helping takes longer than just processing), but creates profound impact that compounds over time through relationships and reputation.

Uniqueness: Being Authentically You

In a world of AI-generated everything, being genuinely yourself becomes increasingly valuable. But what does that mean practically?

The Authenticity Practice:

1. Know what makes you different

Not better, just different. What's your unusual combination of experiences, perspectives, and values? What do you notice that others miss? What do you care about that others overlook?

Write this down. Literally. *"I'm the person who combines climate science with finance with experience in emerging economies with commitment to community wellbeing."* That specific combination is yours.

2. Lead with your difference

When starting a project, writing content, or approaching any work, begin from your unique perspective rather than trying to sound like everyone else.

Don't ask *"What would a consultant say about this?"* Ask *"What do I see about this that others might miss?"*

3. Resist template thinking

AI excels at templates. It can produce standard consultant-speak, standard marketing copy, standard everything. If you're competing on template quality, AI will beat you.

Your value comes from what doesn't fit templates: your specific insights, your particular way of explaining things, your authentic voice.

A Monthly Check:

Once a month, review your work output. How much of it could have been produced by someone else using the same tools? How much is distinctly yours?

If the ratio is concerning (most could have been someone else), recommit to leading with your uniqueness.

Connecting to dimensions: Uniqueness primarily drives perception (you're remembered and sought out specifically) and impact (your specific perspective creates insights others wouldn't generate), while utility comes from the value of that unique perspective rather than from volume or speed.

Ethics: Holding the Line Daily

Ethics isn't about big dramatic moments. It's about small choices made consistently when no one is watching.

The Daily Ethics Check:

Before any significant decision or action, ask:

"If this decision appeared on the front page of the newspaper tomorrow, would I be proud or embarrassed?"

If embarrassed, that's your conscience speaking. Listen to it.

"Would I want my children (or someone I mentor) to make this same choice?"

What you model shapes others. Model what you want to see in the world.

"Ten years from now, will I be glad I made this choice?"

Short-term gains often become long-term regrets. Long-term integrity often requires short-term sacrifice.

Specific AI Ethics Practices:

Before deploying AI in your work, ask:

- Have I tested this for bias or unintended consequences?
- Am I being transparent about AI's role?
- If this causes harm, do I have a plan to address it?
- Am I using AI to serve genuine needs or just to appear cutting-edge?

When tempted to use AI to cut corners:

- Will this compromise the quality or trustworthiness of my work?
- Am I hiding AI use because I know it would undermine perception of value?
- Would I be comfortable explaining exactly how I used AI to produce this?

A Weekly Practice:

Each week, identify one moment when you held to ethics despite pressure or temptation. Celebrate it. You reinforced who you are.

Then identify one moment when you compromised. What made you compromise? What will you do differently next time? No shame, just learning.

Connecting to dimensions: Ethics undergirds all three dimensions. It maintains perception (people trust you because you're consistently ethical), ensures utility serves genuine needs (not just optimizes metrics), and determines whether impact is positive or extractive.

Living with Intention in an AI-Infused Society

The V.A.L.U.E. Framework provides structure. But living it requires a deeper commitment to intentionality in a world designed to capture your attention and automate your choices.

The Practice of Noticing

Start by noticing when you're interacting with AI. Not to avoid it, but to be conscious of it.

When your social media feed surfaces content, notice: What's it showing me? What's it not showing me? How is this shaping what I think matters?

When an algorithm recommends a product, notice: Why this suggestion? What assumptions is it making about me? Do I actually need this, or am I being nudged toward a purchase?

When AI assists your work, notice: What am I letting it do? What am I keeping in my control? Am I developing my capabilities or atrophying them?

This isn't paranoia. It's consciousness. You can't make intentional choices about things you don't notice.

Designing Your Environment for Intentional Living

You're not going to opt out of AI. That ship has sailed. But you can be deliberate about how you engage with it.

Choose tools that align with your values. Some AI services prioritize user wellbeing. Others optimize for engagement at any cost. These aren't equivalent choices. Be deliberate about which you use.

Set boundaries around automation. Just because something can be automated doesn't mean it should be. Maybe you want to write birthday cards by hand even though AI could do it. Maybe you want to plan your route yourself sometimes even though the algorithm is more efficient. These *"inefficiencies"* are choices to remain engaged with your life.

Create spaces free from AI mediation. Times and places where you're not being tracked, predicted, or optimized. Where you can think without recommendation, create without template, connect without algorithm. These spaces become increasingly precious as AI becomes increasingly pervasive.

Choosing Value Over Vanity: A Daily Discipline

The AI age throws vanity metrics at you constantly. Followers. Likes. Views. Downloads. Rankings. Comparisons.

These metrics are designed to be addictive. They give you little dopamine hits while pulling your attention away from what actually matters.

The Vanity Trap in the AI Age

Vanity metrics measure visibility and popularity. Value metrics measure impact and contribution.

You can have millions of followers and create no value. You can have twelve loyal customers and change their lives.

You can be famous and empty. You can be unknown and full of purpose.

The trap is that vanity metrics are visible and social, while value metrics are often private and slow to reveal themselves. It's easier to count likes than to measure lives changed. It's easier to track revenue than to assess whether you're actually helping people.

AI makes vanity metrics easier to achieve and less meaningful. You can buy followers, generate content at scale, game algorithms. But none of this creates real value.

Meanwhile, AI makes genuine value creation harder to measure but more impactful when achieved. Using AI to actually help people, to solve real problems, to create beauty or meaning creates compound effects that don't show up in analytics dashboards.

Staying Grounded: Practical Steps

Define your own metrics. Don't let platforms or society tell you what success looks like. Decide for yourself what would constitute a life well-lived, work well-done. Write it down. Refer to it regularly.

What matters to you? Not what should matter, but what actually does. For me, it's whether clients' situations genuinely improve because of my work, whether I'm building knowledge and capability that serves future challenges, whether I'm treating people with dignity regardless of what they can do for me.

Your metrics might be different. What's important is that they're yours and they measure actual value, not just visible success.

Seek feedback from people you serve. Not likes or ratings. Actual conversations about whether you're helping and how you could help more.

Once a quarter, ask three people you've served: *"What value did I create for you? What could I have done better? What do you still need help with?"*

These conversations are uncomfortable. They also provide the most valuable feedback you'll ever receive.

Celebrate invisible wins. The client who doesn't leave you a testimonial but whose business is thriving. The student who doesn't tag you on social media but whose life changed because of something you taught them. These matter more than public recognition.

Keep a private log of these wins. Not to share on LinkedIn, but to remind yourself what you're actually building when vanity metrics feel discouraging.

Accept obscurity. You might do your best work and never get credit for it. That's not just okay, it's often the reality of genuine contribution. Make peace with it.

Personal Legacy and Societal Contribution

You're going to die. Not soon, hopefully. But definitely. Everyone you know is going to die. The organizations you build will eventually dissolve. The products you create will become obsolete.

This isn't morbid. It's the most clarifying truth there is. Given that everything is temporary, what matters? What endures?

Your Actual Legacy

Your legacy is what lives on after you're gone. Not your bank account. Not your job title. Your influence on people.

Did you help someone discover their potential? Did you create something that made life better for others? Did you treat people with dignity even when it cost you something? Did you stand for something worth standing for?

These questions are legacy questions. And they're available to everyone, not just people with resources or platform or position.

The barista who remembers regular customers' names and asks about their lives creates legacy. The teacher who sees potential in a struggling student and invests extra time creates legacy. The engineer who insists on ethical design even when pushed for speed creates legacy.

Legacy isn't about scale. It's about depth. It's about the quality of your presence and contribution, not the quantity of your accomplishments.

The Societal Level

Individual contribution matters, but so does engaging with larger systems and structures.

The AI transformation we're living through isn't just a technological shift. It's a societal restructuring that will reshape work, education, economics, and power distribution.

You can't control this transformation, but you can influence it. Not necessarily through high-level policy, though some people will work there. Most influence happens through thousands of small choices about how to build, how to treat people, how to use power.

Every time you choose transparency over opacity, you influence norms. Every time you prioritize human wellbeing over algorithmic efficiency, you send a signal about what matters. Every time you speak up about something that doesn't sit right, you create space for others to do the same.

You're not just creating value in your own work. You're contributing to the larger question of what kind of AI-infused society we want to become.

Integration: The Daily Question

Here's a practice to integrate everything we've discussed:

At the end of each day, ask yourself: *"Did I create value today?"*

Not *"Was I productive?"* Not *"Did I succeed?"* Simply: *"Did I create value?"*

Then break it down across our three dimensions:

Utility: Did my work function well? Did it solve the problem it was meant to solve? Did I use tools (including AI) effectively?

Perception: Did I build trust? Did people experience me as authentic and genuinely invested in helping them? Did my actions align with my stated values?

Impact: Did my work make a positive difference? Not just complete a task, but contribute to something meaningful? Did it serve human flourishing or just serve metrics?

Some days the answer will be a clear yes across all dimensions. You helped someone. You made progress on meaningful work. You treated people with dignity. You learned something important.

Some days the answer will be no. You went through motions. You chased metrics. You cut corners. You prioritized urgency over importance.

Most days will be somewhere between.

The question isn't for judgment. It's for awareness. It's a gentle recalibration toward what matters.

Over time, asking this question daily reshapes your choices. You start noticing opportunities to create value that you would have missed before. You start saying no to things that look productive but aren't actually valuable. You start aligning your daily actions with your deeper intentions.

The Long Game: Building a Life of Value

Creating value as a lifestyle isn't about perfection. You'll mess up. You'll have days or weeks where you drift. You'll make choices you regret.

That's fine. This is a practice, not a test. The question is always *"What's my next choice?"* not *"Have I failed?"*

Every moment is a chance to recalibrate. Every day is a chance to create value. Every interaction is a chance to treat someone with dignity. Every decision is a chance to choose ethics over expediency.

You're not trying to be perfect. You're trying to be intentional. You're trying to live in alignment with what you actually believe matters.

And here's what happens over a lifetime of small choices made with intention: you become someone who creates genuine value. Not occasionally, but consistently. Not as a role, but as an identity.

The V.A.L.U.E. Framework isn't just a tool for business decisions. It's a lens for seeing your entire life:

Vision keeps you oriented toward what matters most.

Augmentation helps you use tools without being used by them.

Love ensures your work serves genuine human needs.

Uniqueness keeps you authentic in a world of artificial everything.

Ethics maintains your integrity when pressure mounts to compromise.

And across all of this, the three dimensions of value (utility, perception, impact) help you assess whether you're actually creating value or just staying busy.

The work you do matters. The relationships you build matter. The way you treat people matters. The stand you take matters. The beauty you create matters. The service you offer matters.

Not because someone is keeping score. But because that's what a life well-lived looks like.

As we move to the conclusion, the question isn't whether you've learned enough. It's whether you'll begin. Tomorrow morning. With the practices we've discussed. With imperfect action. With courage to create value in a world that desperately needs what only humans can offer: judgment, wisdom, care, and purpose-driven contribution.

The AI age doesn't diminish the value of a well-lived life. It amplifies it. Because in a world of artificial intelligence, authentic humanity becomes the ultimate premium.

After Efficiency

Conclusion

The Human Spirit in the Age of Algorithms

I decided to found Climate Platform during the COVID pandemic because my boss asked me to risk my life for business convenience. That moment forced a reckoning: What am I actually building with my life? What value am I creating? And for whom?

As I wrote in the introduction, a client later called to warn me that AI could soon make me irrelevant. That warning could have paralyzed me. Instead, it forced me to grapple with the deepest questions about value, contribution, and what it means to be human when intelligence itself is no longer uniquely ours.

This book is the result of that grappling. Not a finished answer, but a framework for navigating uncertainty. Not certainty about the future, but clarity about what endures.

The Journey from Fear to Framework

When I lost my first tender after founding Climate Platform, the anxiety was overwhelming. I'd overestimated my value. The market didn't agree with my self-assessment. I had to adjust my fees, rebuild my confidence, and prove my worth through demonstrated impact rather than assumed expertise.

Then, when I faced that climate finance study, I had to choose: maximize efficiency by using AI to do everything myself, or invest in human expertise that would create better outcomes but reduce my margin. I chose people. That choice, and the success it generated, taught me something fundamental.

Value isn't created by choosing humans over AI or AI over humans. Value is created by orchestrating both to serve genuine needs in ways neither could alone.

This insight became the foundation of everything in this book:

Value = [(AI Utility × Human Judgment) × Perception] + Impact

When AI utility and human judgment multiply together, they create potential. When that potential is perceived as trustworthy and authentic, it multiplies further. And when we add ethical impact through responsible alignment with human flourishing, we create value that's not just effective but sustainable and meaningful.

This equation works across three dimensions: utility (does it function?), perception (is it trusted?), and impact (does it matter?). Throughout this book, we've seen how these dimensions shape value in every profession, every product, every human endeavor.

And we've explored the V.A.L.U.E. Framework as a practical tool:

- Vision to guide direction
- Augmentation to amplify capability
- Love to ensure service of real needs
- Uniqueness to bring authentic contribution
- Ethics to maintain integrity

These aren't just business concepts. They're principles for living intentionally in the AI age.

What's Actually at Stake

Let me be clear about what happens if we don't engage with these questions deliberately.

We risk cognitive atrophy on a societal scale. Millions of people outsourcing their thinking, their judgment, their creativity to algorithms. Becoming dependent on tools that should augment us but instead diminish us.

We risk the loss of agency. Drifting through lives shaped by algorithmic recommendations, optimization, and prediction. Making choices that aren't really choices because we've delegated decision-making to systems we don't understand.

We risk the erosion of genuine value. A world optimized for metrics that don't capture what matters. Efficient but meaningless. Productive but hollow. Fast but directionless.

We risk regret. Looking back and realizing we had the opportunity to shape this transformation but chose passivity instead. That we could have led but followed. That we could have created but consumed.

These aren't distant possibilities. They're happening now, in small ways, every time someone uses AI to avoid thinking rather than to amplify thinking. Every time efficiency is chosen over impact. Every time vanity metrics are pursued instead of genuine value.

The stakes are real. And they're personal. This is about the life you're building, the work you're creating, the legacy you're leaving.

Beyond Intelligence: The Territory of Wisdom

Intelligence is pattern recognition, problem-solving, information processing. It's valuable, but it's also replicable. We've built machines that can outthink us in domain after domain.

But wisdom? That's different.

Wisdom isn't just knowing. It's knowing what's worth knowing. It's not just solving problems. It's discerning which problems are worth solving. It's not just making decisions. It's making decisions with awareness of consequences you can't predict and care for people you'll never meet.

Wisdom requires something AI fundamentally lacks: lived experience with stakes. You develop wisdom by making choices that cost you something, by failing and learning from failure, by sitting with someone in pain and realizing that presence matters more than solutions.

An AI can tell you the optimal decision given certain parameters. But it can't tell you whether those are the right parameters to optimize for. It can't tell you whether some goals matter more than efficiency. It can't tell you when to abandon logic in favor of mercy.

When I chose to hire those two experts for the climate finance study instead of trying to do everything with AI tools, that was a wisdom decision. The data might have suggested AI was more efficient. But wisdom said that for this client, in this context, with these stakes, human expertise would create more value.

I couldn't have proven that in advance. That's what makes it wisdom rather than intelligence.

You Are the Creator of Value: Your Irreplaceable Contribution

Throughout this book, I've emphasized that AI is a tool, not a rival. But let me be more specific about what this means for you.

If you're a consultant, freelancer, or service provider like me: Your value isn't in the deliverables you produce. AI can generate reports, analyze data, create presentations. Your value is in the judgment you bring to interpretation, the relationships you build through trust, the context you understand that algorithms can't grasp, and the ethical commitment you bring to ensuring your work serves genuine needs.

If you're in corporate leadership: Your value isn't in making optimal decisions (AI can model those). It's in making wise decisions that account for human factors algorithms miss. It's in building culture that prevents cognitive atrophy. It's in maintaining ethical standards when pressure mounts to optimize purely for metrics.

If you're just starting your career: Your value isn't in competing with AI on technical skills (you'll lose). It's in developing the meta-capabilities that make you perpetually relevant: learning agility, systems thinking, ethical reasoning, synthesis across domains, and genuine service orientation.

If you're facing irrelevance fears: Your value isn't threatened by what AI can do. It's threatened by failing to develop what only you can bring: your unique combination of experiences, perspectives, and care shaped by your unrepeatable life.

You possess something no algorithm can replicate: the specific lens through which you see the world, shaped by your particular journey. When you bring your full humanity to your work, when you allow your unique perspective to shape what you build and who you serve, you create value that literally cannot be replicated.

Not because you're doing something technically impressive, but because you're doing something that could only come from you.

What You Can Do Tomorrow Morning

Theory without action remains theory. Here's what creating value in the AI age actually looks like in practice:

Tomorrow morning, before checking your phone:

1. **Set vision for the day. Ask:** *"What value do I want to create today?"* Be specific. Write it down.

2. **Identify your augmentation strategy. Ask:** *"What will I let AI do, what will I keep human, and what will we do together?"* Make conscious choices rather than defaulting to whatever's easiest.

3. Choose one person to genuinely serve. Not just provide a service to, but actually understand and help. Let love (genuine service) guide at least one interaction.

This week:

1. Do one significant piece of work without AI assistance. Keep your cognitive muscles strong. Don't let them atrophy.

2. Have one conversation focused purely on understanding someone else's needs. Not to pitch, not to sell, but to genuinely understand. Practice empathy as a skill.

3. Make one choice based on ethics rather than efficiency. Even if it costs you something. Build the muscle of integrity.

This month:

1. Review your work through the three dimensions. Is it high utility (does it function well)? Does it build perception (trust and authenticity)? Does it create positive impact (genuine value, not just metrics)?

2. Assess yourself against the V.A.L.U.E. Framework. Where are you strong? Where are you weak? What needs development?

3. Invest in your uniqueness. What makes you different? Double down on it rather than trying to be like everyone else.

This year:

Commit to becoming more human, not less. As AI handles more technical work, invest in developing wisdom, judgment, empathy, ethical reasoning, and genuine care for others.

These aren't grand gestures. They're small practices that compound over time into a life of value creation.

A Call to Courage, Curiosity, and Co-Creation

We're living through a transformation as significant as the industrial revolution. The structure of work, the nature of contribution, the meaning of value, all of it is being renegotiated in real time.

This is terrifying. I won't pretend otherwise. I feel it every time a new AI capability emerges that can do something I thought was uniquely human. Every time I wonder whether Climate Platform will still be relevant in five years. Every time I question whether the skills I've spent decades developing still matter.

But it's also thrilling. Because moments of transformation are when the future is most malleable. The choices we make now, the values we embed now, the systems we build now will shape decades to come.

You have agency in this moment. Not total control. But real influence.

I'm calling you to courage. Not the courage of certainty, knowing you're right. But the courage of commitment, choosing to act in service of what matters even when the outcome is uncertain.

Courage to choose ethics over expediency. Courage to prioritize long-term flourishing over short-term gain. Courage to build things that serve real human needs rather than just optimizing metrics. Courage to be fully present with other humans even when mediation through screens and algorithms is easier.

Courage to begin before you're ready, to act despite fear, to create value in a world changing faster than any of us can fully comprehend.

I'm calling you to curiosity. Curiosity about how AI actually works, demystifying it so you can use it wisely. Curiosity about how others are adapting, learning from their experiments. Curiosity about your own assumptions, questioning whether what you think you know is actually true.

Most importantly, curiosity about people. The humans you serve, the humans you work with, the humans whose lives are disrupted by technology. Genuine curiosity, the kind that makes you ask questions and actually listen to answers, is the antidote to the arrogance and extraction that plague much of the tech world.

I'm calling you to co-creation. The future is neither human-only nor machine-only. It's collaborative. The best outcomes will emerge when we learn to work with AI in ways that amplify human wisdom rather than replace it.

But this requires discernment. You need to know when to trust the algorithm and when to override it. When to accept efficiency and when to insist on something slower and more human. When to scale and when to stay small and personal.

There's no formula for this. It's judgment you develop through practice, through mistakes, through paying attention to outcomes both intended and unintended.

What Gives Me Hope

Despite everything I've shared about risks and challenges, I'm fundamentally hopeful about our future.

Not because I think AI will solve all our problems. It won't. Not because I think humans will automatically make good choices. We won't always.

But because I've seen what happens when people bring their full humanity to their work in the AI age.

I've seen consultants using AI to augment their analysis while deepening their client relationships through genuine care and understanding.

I've seen leaders maintaining ethical standards even when pressure mounts to optimize purely for efficiency.

I've seen young professionals developing wisdom and judgment while learning to use powerful tools responsibly.

I've seen entrepreneurs building businesses that create genuine value while using AI to amplify their impact.

When I chose to hire those experts instead of relying purely on AI, the outcome exceeded my expectations not because we rejected technology, but because we orchestrated human and machine capabilities wisely. That experience taught me that the future isn't about choosing sides. It's about choosing integration, guided by wisdom and ethics.

This is happening everywhere, in small ways, by people who've decided to lead rather than drift. Who've chosen to create value rather than just extract it. Who've committed to being more human, not less, in an age of machines.

That's what gives me hope. Not grand predictions about technology, but ordinary people making extraordinary choices about how to use their agency.

The Invitation: Your Choice, Your Future

You've reached the end of this book, but you're at the beginning of your own journey with these questions.

The value you create in the AI age won't come from reading about it. It will come from living into it. From making choices day by day, project by project, relationship by relationship that align with what you believe matters.

Some of those choices will work beautifully. You'll find ways to use AI that amplify your impact beyond what you imagined possible. You'll create value that serves real needs and builds real trust.

Some of those choices won't work. You'll waste time on tools that don't fit your workflow. You'll trust AI when you should have trusted your judgment. You'll optimize metrics that turn out not to matter.

Both outcomes are valuable. Success shows you what's possible. Failure teaches you what's essential.

What matters is that you stay engaged. That you don't retreat into denial about how fast things are changing. That you don't surrender your agency to algorithms. That you keep asking what value means and how you can create it.

Consider what you want your work to be about, not just what you want it to produce. Consider who you want to serve and why their flourishing matters to you. Consider what you're willing to stand for even when it costs you something.

These aren't questions you answer once. They're questions you live with. But having them as your companions, letting them guide your choices, that's what transforms work from a means of survival into a source of meaning.

The Human Spirit Endures

Here's what I believe, and it's the deepest conviction I have:

The human spirit, our capacity for love and creativity and courage and wisdom, our ability to find meaning in suffering and beauty in chaos, our stubborn insistence on dignity and justice and connection, this doesn't diminish as machines get smarter.

If anything, it becomes more precious. More necessary. More powerful.

Because in the end, what we're building with AI isn't just technology. It's the future of human civilization. And that future will be shaped not by the algorithms we write but by the values we encode, the priorities we set, the choices we make about what matters.

You're part of shaping that future. Whether you're building products or raising children, leading organizations or teaching students, writing code or creating art, every day you're making choices that influence what comes next.

Make those choices well. Make them with intention. Make them with care for people you'll never meet and consequences you can't fully predict.

Make them human.

Because that's what the age of algorithms needs most. Not people trying to be more like machines. But people willing to be courageously, compassionately, wisely human.

That's where value lives. That's where meaning endures. That's where the future we actually want to inhabit gets built.

One choice at a time. One day at a time. One human connecting with another, seeing each other's dignity, serving each other's flourishing.

AI will keep advancing. Technology will keep transforming everything. The pace won't slow.

But the human spirit? That's not going anywhere. It's been here since we first gathered around fires to tell stories. It's survived every technological revolution. And it will outlast this one too.

Not because we're resisting change. But because we're bringing our full humanity to it.

That's the work. That's the invitation. That's the value only you can create.

Tomorrow morning, when you wake up, you have a choice. You can drift into reactive mode, letting algorithms and urgencies shape your day. Or you can set intention, choose augmentation wisely, serve genuine needs, bring your uniqueness, and hold to your ethics.

That choice, repeated daily, compounds into a life of value. Into work that matters. Into contribution that endures.

The AI age doesn't diminish the value of a well-lived life. It amplifies it. Because in a world of artificial intelligence, authentic humanity becomes the ultimate premium.

Go build something beautiful. Something that serves real needs. Something that reflects your unique perspective. Something that makes the world incrementally better.

The future is waiting for you to help create it.

And I, for one, am grateful you're willing to try.

ACKNOWLEDGMENTS

This book exists because people I serve asked questions I couldn't answer with what I knew. Their curiosity and concern pushed me to think more deeply about value, meaning, and contribution in our current fast changing world.

It is written for anyone navigating the uncertainties of the AI age: the entrepreneur facing visible risk, the young professional wondering how long relevance lasts, the experienced leader seeking to empower others.

"After Efficiency" is for those who want to stay useful, responsible, and purposeful while the rules are being rewritten.

About the Author

Pierre Telep is a strategic advisor and founder of Climate Platform, a consulting firm dedicated to unlocking climate-related value in emerging economies. With a background spanning engineering, climate finance, and international development, Pierre has spent two decades at the intersection of sustainability and innovation.

His work has taken him across Africa, Asia, Europe, and beyond, advising governments, NGOs, and businesses on how to align economic development with environmental responsibility. He's seen firsthand how technology transforms communities, how good intentions can create unintended consequences, and how the choices we make today ripple into futures we'll never see.

This book grew from a personal crisis: being told his expertise might soon be obsolete. Rather than retreat into denial or despair, Pierre chose to investigate what value means in an age where intelligence itself becomes abundant. The result is a framework for creating meaningful impact that transcends any particular technology or trend.

He lives with his family in Berlin, where he continues to consult, write, and wrestle with questions about how we build a future worth inheriting. He can be reached through Climate Platform's website or on LinkedIn, where he shares ongoing reflections on value creation in the AI age.

His next project is already taking shape: exploring how communities can navigate technological transformation while preserving what makes them human. If you're wrestling with similar questions, he'd love to hear from you.

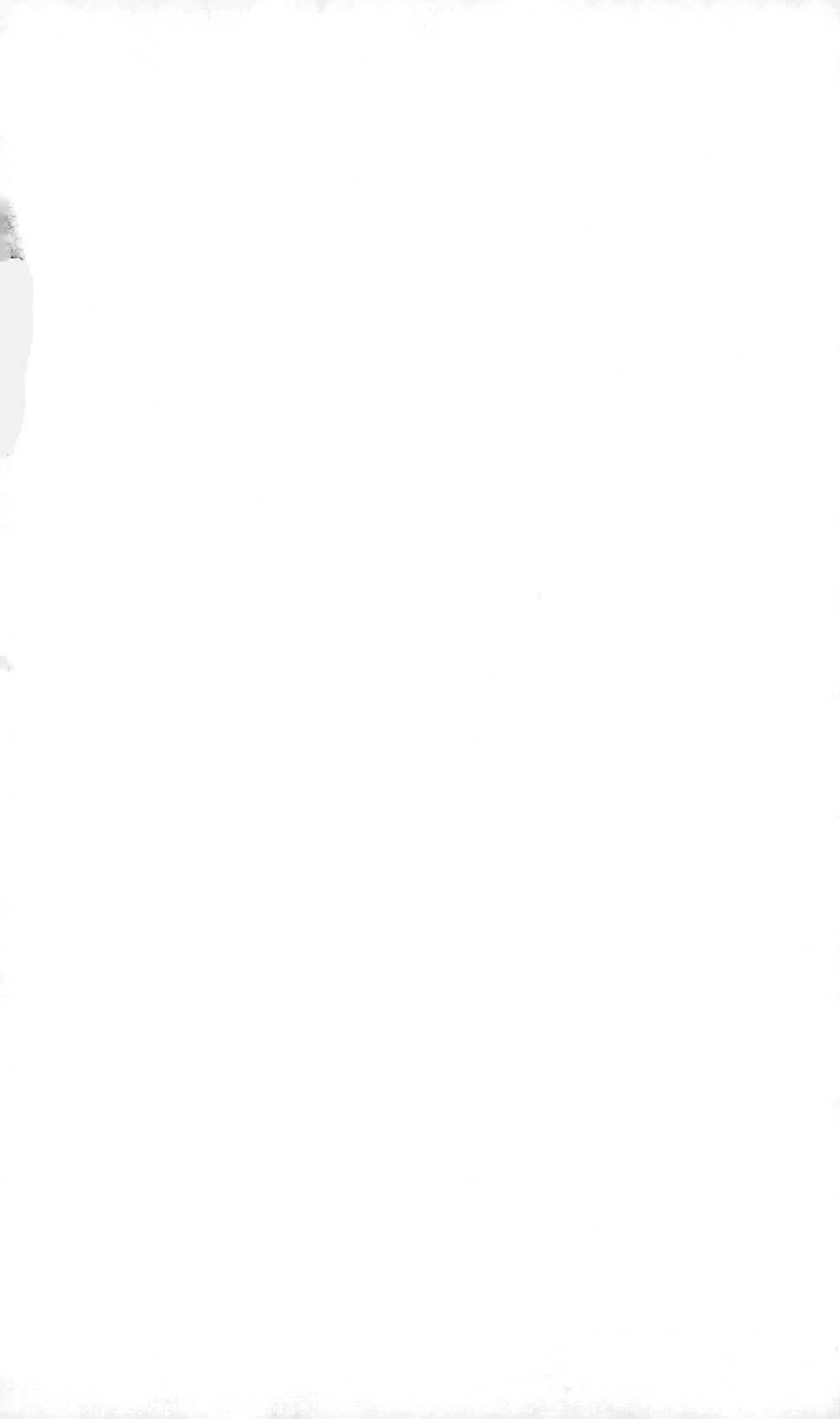

www.ingramcontent.com/pod-product-compliance
Lightning Source LLC
Chambersburg PA
CBHW071556200326
41519CB00021BB/6769